D1179091

AMERIKE

The Briton Who Gave America its Name

AMERIKE

The Briton Who Gave America its Name

R O D N E Y   B R O O M E

SUTTON PUBLISHING

First published in 2002 by
Sutton Publishing Limited · Phoenix Mill
Thrupp · Stroud · Gloucestershire · GL5 2BU

British Library Cataloguing in Publication Data
A catalogue record for this book is available from the British
Library

ISBN 0 7509 2909 X

Typeset in 13/16 pt Perpetua.
Typesetting and origination by
Sutton Publishing Limited.
Printed and bound in England by
J.H. Haynes & Co. Ltd, Sparkford.

CONTENTS

LIST OF ILLUSTRATIONS

List of Illustrations

List of Illustrations

Colour Plate Section between pages 104 and 105

ACKNOWLEDGEMENTS

The chance to write a book like this comes but once in a lifetime. I am grateful for the opportunity afforded me and I would like to thank all the people who have helped and encouraged me.

I particularly wish to thank my cousin Peter Martin, a Bristolian and local history enthusiast. Born in Bristol myself, I have long been aware of the story of Richard Amerike, but at the time I began to show a serious interest in the subject, Peter was already undertaking extensive research and was preparing, with Peter Macdonald, a publication about John Cabot, Richard Amerike and other local families of fifteenth-century Bristol.

After I had begun writing the book, I was fortunate to meet a colleague of Peter's, Anna Hurl, who, during my short holiday in Bristol, kindly gave me access to many of the files, including copies of manuscripts, she had collected on Peter's behalf. The detailed information she provided saved me hours of research and, probably, another trip: my thanks, therefore, to Anna as well.

I would also like to thank another Bristol historian, Anton Bantock (who is acknowledged in almost all the books on Bristol history I consulted); and Hubert Williams (a former Mayor of Bristol) and his daughter Wendy for an illuminating tour of St Mary Redcliffe Church. I am equally indebted to the Master of the *Matthew*, Nigel Ottley, and crew members Shawn and Jean for a below-deck visit of the ship, and to the present owners of Richard Amerike's Ashton-Phillips house, Donna and Steven Brown, who enthusiastically showed me around the house and gave me copies of several important documents, in particular the newspaper article from the *Western Daily Press*.

My thanks also extend to the following: the Reverend Beverly Tasker, vicar of All Saints Church, Long Ashton, who enlightened me on the history of this village where Amerike held property and his descendants are believed to be buried; Lars Haaheim and Martin Lode for their firsthand knowledge of the salt cod and stockfish trade; Kieran O'Mahony, who helped to make this book a reality and Tina Bonfield, who brought us together (US); Karl Pelkan, for his leads on several points; Gerry Brooke of Bristol Evening Post and Press for permission to use the newspaper articles from the *Western Daily Press* and the *Evening Post*; and the Bristol Film and Video Society, for introducing me to the wonderful film, *John Cabot – The Story*, which, for me, brought the account of Richard Amerike to life.

Finally, I would like to thank all the staff at Sutton Publishing, and especially my editor, Jaqueline Mitchell.

PREFACE

The fairest, goodliest and most famous parish church in England.

Queen Elizabeth I, August 1574.[1]

We stood on the gravel path outside St Mary Redcliffe Church, squinting skywards at the towering spire. The pointed edifice cast a ragged shadow across the river and the quays toward Queen Square and the neighbourhood where my father lived when he was young. I didn't know it then, but it would cast an even greater shadow to the west, past the narrow streets, past the spilling tidewater and across the Atlantic to a new world that would one day be my home.

We had been walking at a fast pace through the narrow streets and along the quays of the old city. I can still hear my father's shoes clicking rhythmically on the cobblestones in the nearly deserted streets. It was a Sunday afternoon in the autumn of 1952. I was eight years old at the time. My father had grown up in these streets, and when he looked at the closed businesses and shuttered warehouses, it was with an air of quiet expectation of the activity and commerce that would soon signal the start of another week.

It was foggy, damp and piercingly cold as the wind whistled up from the river. My father called the corner where the River Frome meets the River Avon 'the North Pole', and that is the name by which I have referred to it ever since.

Inside the church he showed me the giant whalebone standing in the small chapel just inside the main doors. I recall it being about twice my height, and we added our fingerprints to the shiny, black surface. Father told me that John Cabot brought this back with him from Newfoundland 500 years ago.

Growing up as a lad in Bristol meant living the legends of the great discoverers and the many other colourful characters of the sea. Edward Teach, the notorious pirate, known as 'Blackbeard', walked these streets, as did the Governor of the Bahamas, Captain Woodes Rogers, who was responsible for Blackbeard's death in a sea battle off the North Carolina coast in 1718. The same Captain Woodes Rogers rescued Alexander Selkirk, a seaman stranded on a Pacific island. Daniel Defoe met them in a waterfront public house in Bristol, and his classic novel, *Robinson Crusoe*, was the result. William Dampier, a buccaneer who later became a famous scientist, and the pirate Henry Morgan were also familiar figures in Bristol's streets. Even Robert Louis Stevenson's fictional Long John Silver reputedly frequented two of Bristol's public houses, which exist to this day.

Merchant ships came right into the city centre, as they had done for hundreds of years. To this hub of mercantile activity fascinating cargoes were delivered daily and business seemed to overflow into the numerous taverns. Sitting on the quayside were casks and barrels of sherry, port and wine just unloaded from the ships. The brewery, situated on the river next to Bristol Bridge, still used horses to draw the beer drays, and the barrels were rolled off noisily and steered down the alleys until they reached the wooden cellar hatches that opened up in the narrow pavements outside the pubs.

The smells of the city changed between the street and the alley, for at the end of every street was the river. The ships' cargoes brought an assortment of sweet and acrid aromas that mixed with the everyday river offering. Fish arrived fresh and bloody in boxes; hops for the brewery were heavy with fragrance; sherry and wine came in foreign casks with romantic Mediterranean names; bananas and rotting food caused the seagulls to make a commotion. Sawdust was sprinkled liberally everywhere so that spillages could be cleaned up regularly. Added to these were the industrial smells of timber, coal, and coal gas, which was manufactured in the works behind the cathedral.

My grandfather was not a native Bristolian. He was born in 1860 and raised in Conwy, a small town on the North Wales coast. As a schoolboy, he would look out to sea at the sailing ships leaving from Liverpool, some 60 miles to the east along the coast. Many of these ships were sailing to America. The sea was in his blood, and within a few years, he moved to South Wales and then to Bristol. In December 1899, he gained his Master Mariner's certificate, and he entered the new century as the captain of his first ship.

Between 1896 and 1900 he sailed on a merchant sailing ship called the *Morven*. In the first decade of the twentieth century he captained two other merchant ships, the *Menantic* and the *Mohican*, which sailed between Bristol and the United States. After the outbreak of the First World War he delivered petroleum products to France. I still imagine him crossing the Atlantic under sail to Canada, hauling Welsh coal outbound and Canadian wheat back to Bristol. He was a member of the Society of Merchant Venturers, the organization that took care of my grandmother and the children's education after he died in 1917. My father spoke very highly of this body.

Their house was situated on the quay itself, where the merchant ships moored, and just across the river from St Mary Redcliffe Church, reputed to be the most magnificent parish church in England. Much of the church dates from the thirteenth century and

Canynges's reconstruction, but the spire was built in 1859 to replace the one that crashed down onto the nave in 1445, having been hit by lightning. St Mary Redcliffe was the merchants' church, and some of the people mentioned in this book are buried here.

St Mary Redcliffe Church, Bristol: the merchants' church. (*Photograph courtesy of Lesley Nicholls*)

My father and his brother both attended St Nicholas Church primary school, which was just a quarter of mile's walk from the house across the street from Bristol Bridge. St Nicholas's is the sailors' church.

As children growing up in Bristol, we knew about John Cabot, whose statue stands in front of the Council House. Likewise, we had heard of the *Matthew*, the ship that took him to North America. My father also related stories of the Bristol fish traders who went as far as Newfoundland years earlier.

Bristol, with its westward perspective, has always had strong connections with America. Before the Revolution in 1776 60 per cent of all trade passing through Bristol was destined for or from the American colonies. The first United States Consulate was opened in Bristol in 1792, even before the country was accorded an embassy in London: the wheels of trade were more important than political niceties.

In 1897, Bristol commemorated the 400th anniversary of John Cabot's voyage in the *Matthew*, when he supposedly became the first European to set foot on American soil. The focus provided by the festival preparations caused the unearthing of many new pieces of evidence that, when pieced together, promised a tantalizing story surrounding the events that took place toward the end of the 1400s. The discovery of a letter in Spain in 1955 and shipping records in London in the 1960s have considerably strengthened the evidence supporting what had long been suspected regarding the discovery and naming of America. A hundred years later, in 1997, the city of Bristol reconstructed a replica of the *Matthew* and followed Cabot's journey to Newfoundland.

Four years ago when I first began working on this story, I gave little thought to my retracing my grandfather's journey from the quay in Bristol across the Mare Oceanum to America; and I had no idea that this journey through time would lead me to my own roots in North Wales.

To my grandfather, Captain William Broome
and my father, Cecil Broome

INTRODUCTION

Terra Incognita, the fourth continent, lay dormant, as if shrouded in a fog, until the year 1502. The indigenous peoples of the continent, the Inuit, Micmac, Aztec, Inca and the Apache, had all built sophisticated societies, but they did not share the ambitions of the Eurocentric world that had expanded to encompass Africa and Asia.

Visitors had been to the shores of *Terra Incognita* before. On arrival, crews disembarked from their ships to accomplish what they had come to do: they cut down trees, fished, settled for the season and then left.

What was different about Christopher Columbus's arrival at the Caribbean Islands in 1492 and, five years later, John Cabot's voyage to New England and Nova Scotia, was that neither man was interested in the land he had reached. They both had further ambitions: both were aiming for Asia.

Naturally, they were frustrated because they could not get around the vast landmass that blocked their way. Columbus was trying to reach India and Cabot, China, and in fact both men believed they had almost reached their destinations. But it was the political opportunism of others that elevated their voyages into 'discoveries'.

Earlier visits to *Terra Incognita* had occurred well before the time of a rapidly expanding international economy. According to legend, an Irish monk arrived there over a thousand years ago. Later, Icelandic and Norwegian wayfarers visited in the tenth century and stayed for about twenty years. Portuguese sailors were reputed to have visited the Caribbean in 1424 and again in the 1470s. Basques most likely reached Newfoundland in the late 1400s and a Dane claimed to have discovered it in 1472. Merchant fishermen from England visited many times from approximately 1480 onward.

Most of the explorers involved in the discovery of the Americas in the late 1400s either knew or were known to each other; in fact their paths crossed, sometimes more than once. The only person who did not meet any of the protagonists was a map-maker who took his last name from his geographical surroundings: Martin Waldseemüller. Ironically, Waldseemüller's fluid pen and the timely invention of movable type had a lasting effect on the way we view our world today: the confluence of a series of historical coincidences would distort and influence our world to a degree out of all proportion to their significance.

It was Waldseemüller who placed the name America on his world map and who made the connection between the word America and the name Amerigo, the first name of Amerigo Vespucci, the explorer whose works he used in compiling his map. It was purely supposition on Waldseemüller's part to make this connection, an educated guess which he acknowledges in the booklet accompanying his map.

It was not until 400 years later that new light was shed on this matter. A document was discovered in the records held at Westminster Abbey that introduced a character whose name was uncannily close to the name America. On the strength of this evidence, a Bristol historian, Mr Alfred Hudd, suggested that America might have been named not after Amerigo Vespucci, as was the conventional wisdom, but after Richard Amerike, a man who had several years earlier been identified as the King's Customs Officer who had paid the pension of the explorer John Cabot in 1497 and 1498.

In 1929 an effort was made to interest the American government in this subject. Bristol's morning newspaper, the *Western Daily Press*, printed a lengthy obituary and a full transcript of Hudd's lecture. The following is an extract from the paper, dated 7 August 1929:

> Recent references to the origin of the name given to the New World discovered by John Cabot in the Bristol ship Matthew, has aroused such widespread interest that we publish in full Mr. A.E. Hudd's paper on the subject.
>
> . . . .

As already stated, the American Consul, Mr. Digby A. Willson, is greatly interested, and has asked for all the evidence available to submit to the appropriate authorities in the United States.

This and many other indications of interest in the subject, suggested that the publication of Mr. Hudd's statement in full, will encourage exhaustive inquiry into a matter of considerable importance to Bristol.

The full text of Mr. Alfred E. Hudd's address . . . is herewith given. [Following is a partial extract of the lecture.]

. . . There is no longer any doubt on the return of [Cabot's] second voyage John received for the second time the handsome [*sic*] pension conferred upon him by the King, from the hands of the Collectors of Customs of the Port of Bristol. One of these officials, the senior of the two, who probably was the person who actually handed over the money to the explorer, was named Richard Ameryk (also written Ap Meryke in one deed) who seems to have been a leading citizen of Bristol at the time, and

'The Naming of America', *Western Daily Press*.

was Sheriff in 1503. Now it has been suggested both by Mr. Scott and myself that the name given to the newly-found land by the discoverer was "Amerika," in honour of the official from whom he received his pension. . . .

Evidently, the United States government was contacted in 1929 regarding the Amerike theory. Perhaps the 1929 stock market crash, the Depression, and ultimately the Second World War, relegated this item to the back burner.

Gradually more evidence came to light, adding fuel to Hudd's original thesis (see Chapter 16). Discoveries continue to be made. In March 2002 Mr Gavin Menzies introduced his revolutionary, China First, theory that a Chinese exploration fleet circumnavigated the world between 1421 and 1423. At the Royal Geographical Society in London he claimed that Admiral Zheng may have sailed westwards, with a large fleet of ships, via the Indian Ocean and the southern tip of Africa to reach the Caribbean Sea, thus discovering America before returning to China.

Menzies believes that within just a few years maps depicting these discoveries had made their way to Venice and to Portugal. He was shown a planosphere in Venice dated to 1459 depicting South Africa and the Cape of Good Hope.

The virtual certainty that Columbus had a 'secret map' prior to 1492, and the fact that Waldseemüller's map of 1507 shows far more detailed knowledge than could ever have been learned from Columbus and Vespucci, is part of the story of this book. Could this new China First theory have provided some of the incentive for Columbus, Cabot and Vespucci, all men from Northern Italy, to reach out across the Atlantic with the confidence that they would succeed in their endeavours?

Many people were involved in the discovery, mapping and naming of America; and many people today are still unaware of the possibility of Amerike's, and Bristol's, role in this. This book, acknowledging and building on this new research, unravels the links between Amerike, Cabot and Columbus, and reveals how this previously little-known trader may have come to be involved in the pioneering discovery of New Founde Lands.

ONE

TWELVE WOODEN PLATES

It is well here to consider the injury and injustice which that Amerigo Vespucci appears to have done to the Admiral [Columbus] ... in attributing the discovery of this continent to himself ... Owing to this, all of the foreigners who write of these Indies in Latin ... call the continent America, as having been first discovered by Amerigo. For as Amerigo was a Latinist, and eloquent, he knew how to make use of the first voyage he undertook, and to give credit to himself, as if he had been the principal captain of it.

Father Bartholomeo de Las Casas,
Bishop of Chiapaz, 1559.[1]

M artin Waldseemüller published a revolutionary world map in 1507, only fifteen years after Columbus landed on the Caribbean Island of San Salvador in the Bahamas. It was the first map to show the Americas as a separate continent. On this map the word America was written across the part of the continent we now call Brazil. It was produced and printed by a group of men working in the Benedictine monastery of St Dié, in a small town located in the Vosges Mountains near Strasbourg, Lorraine, then an independent principality between Germany and France.

In 1505, the Duke of Lorraine, Rene II, engaged Waldseemüller to oversee the production of the map.

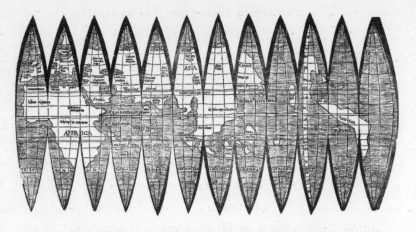

Waldseemüller's map gores, 1507. (*Bell Library, University of Minnesota*)

Waldseemüller was thirty-four years old at that time, an accomplished cosmographer, and a practising cartographer with considerable experience in woodblock printing. In 1500 the Duke and the Canon of St Dié had formed an intellectual group known as the Gymnasium Vosgense to expand the rudiments of cosmography and geometry. Waldseemüller joined Gautier Lud, secretary to the Duke, his nephew Nicolas Lud, Jean Basin de Sandancourt and Matthias Ringmann, a poet and teacher of Latin and Greek. Gautier Lud was a wealthy man who owned one of the newly invented printing presses. It is no surprise that Waldseemüller, Ringmann and other cartographers were associated with the church of St Dié since the clergy made up the majority of the literate classes and were the chief patrons of the book trade in the years leading up to the Renaissance, and long after.

Waldseemüller was born in the village of Wolfenweiler, near Freiburg, a small town in modern Germany close to both the French and Swiss borders, sometime around 1471. In 1480, the family moved to Freiburg, where his father became a member of the city council in 1490. The same year Waldseemüller became a student at Freiburg University. He had a lively interest in the imagery of names. Early in his career, he reinvented himself as Hylacomylus in an attempt to elevate his stature. Hylacomylus was a stylized translation of his name from the Greek word for wood (German *wald*), the Latin for lake, *lacus* (German *see*), and the Greek for mill (German *müller*).[2]

His accomplice, Matthias Ringmann, who is believed to have been responsible for the text, was born in 1482 in Eichhoffen, a village in the vineyards of Alsace between Obernai and Sélestat. He studied in Heidelberg and Paris, becoming proficient in Greek, mathematics, geography, philosophy, poetry, and cosmography. In 1500 he moved to Strasbourg and worked in publishing with Jacques Wimpheling and a printer, Jean Prüss. Academics and humanists often gave themselves Latin names in this period and, accordingly, Ringmann called himself Philesius Vogesigena, Philesius being simply a Latin literary name that occurs in many classical texts, while the

Latinized 'Vogesigena' obviously bears reference to St Dié.[3]

It was well known that the Spanish and Portuguese were exploring southwards along the West African coast and across the Mare Oceanum, but the authorities were secretive about their findings and only revealed details when they were ready to make claim to land. It was 1503 before they released a serious body of information, which was eagerly studied by the cosmographers and cartographers. By this time, Christopher Columbus was on his fourth expedition to the Caribbean. The first was in 1492, and the second was soon after his return, in the following year. During his third voyage, from 1498–1501, he built a large settlement on the island of Hispaniola.

Amerigo Vespucci was an Italian navigator who participated in Columbus's third expedition. Vespucci was born in Florence in March 1454. He was the third son of Ser Nastagio and Simonetta Vespucci, members of an extremely wealthy, aristocratic family who formed part of Florence's ruling elite. He was privately tutored and may have studied under Paolo Toscanelli, the most influential cosmographer of his time.

In 1483 he joined the merchant bank of Lorenzo di Pier Francesco de Medici, who controlled one of Europe's greatest fortunes. This was a relationship that was to last for sixteen years. In 1492 he moved to Seville where he ran the Medici maritime banking office. He was retained by the Spanish King in 1497 to report on Columbus's settlement in the Caribbean. There is much debate as to whether he visited the settlement that year. But he did make other voyages across the Mare Oceanum from Spain or Portugal in 1499, 1501 and 1503.[4]

Vespucci was an educated man who wrote and published books about his voyages. He also sent long detailed letters to Peter Soderini, a boyhood friend in Florence. These letters were published separately.

In 1505, a Latin edition of Vespucci's *Third Voyage* was printed in Strasbourg and was illustrated with woodcut plates. Matthias Ringmann wrote the dedication and a poem. Amerigo Vespucci was evidently aware of the work of the Gymnasium Vosgense, and he may have had frequent communication with the Duke of Lorraine or Ringmann. Ringmann and Waldseemüller obtained the new edition of *The Four Voyages of Amerigo Vespucci*, a published collection of scientific letters and manuscripts he had written to Soderini, and probably accompanying maps. Vespucci may have sent them on himself.[5]

Vespucci planned to produce a world map based on his research, and some think that he communicated this to Ringmann and Waldseemüller. He wrote to his Medici employer that he planned to make two world maps, one a flat page and the other a globe, which is exactly what Waldseemüller did. It is likely that

Vespucci had drawn rudimentary maps and Waldseemüller elaborated upon them.

Duke Rene and Vespucci may have known each other. The Duke had a keen interest in cosmology and visited Toscanelli in Florence in the 1470s while Vespucci was still studying physics and cosmography there as a youth. Vespucci moved to Paris in 1478, where he was attached to the Florentine Embassy; his uncle was Ambassador to Paris. The Duke was known to have visited there.

Strasbourg was the birthplace of the printing industry; Gutenberg set up one of the first printing presses there in 1475. Gutenberg's invention of movable type set in motion a revolution in intellectual opportunism. The Duke of Lorraine and Lud saw the commercial possibilities in producing the most up-to-date world map, the repercussions of which would be far-reaching.

Waldseemüller, who was known for his mapping and his woodcutting skills, started work on the map. He relied on Ptolemy's *Geographia* as the basis for Europe, Africa, and Asia. For his depiction of the eastern coastline of the New World, he faithfully reproduced a map published in 1505 by an Italian map-maker named Nicolo Caveri. In 1502, Alberto Cantino, an Italian diplomat in Lisbon, illegally obtained a Portuguese map of the New World, which he smuggled to his employer, the Duke of Ferrara, Ercole d'Este. Caveri's map duplicated the Cantino map and added details of the coastline in the Gulf of

Mexico. Caveri's map was sent from Italy to Waldseemüller's group by the Medici family.[6]

The remainder of Waldseemüller's map of the New World relied entirely on Vespucci's manuscripts, the *Mundus Novus, The Four Voyages of Amerigo Vespucci* and the Soderini letters.[7]

Waldseemüller's group took two years to prepare the map. It was carved onto twelve large wooden plates for printing. Each plate measured 21 by 30 inches. The individual printed paper sheets were designed to be pasted onto a wall in three rows of four. When assembled, the map measured approximately 8 feet by 4 feet 6 inches, about the size of a blackboard. This map, the first map to show the New World in its entirety, was a window opening onto an ancient mystery. It outlined Europe precisely. The coast of Africa is labelled in great detail while the interior is unmarked, unnamed and unexplored. It originally showed North and South America as two separate continents divided by a narrow gap or strait. The name America is used to designate part of the feathery landmass we now know as South America. The general shape of South America is surprisingly accurate, and the west coast of North America is portrayed as mountainous.

As the map was nearing completion in 1507, information came from Columbus's fourth voyage that he was unable to find the straits at the Cape of Catigara

Waldseemüller's World Map of 1507. (*The British Library*)

through which he would be able to sail on to India. Waldseemüller added a small inset at the top of his world map, correctly showing the isthmus between North and South America with no gap. He apparently had information that there was another large ocean on the other side of a narrow isthmus. From his own travels Columbus could not have known of the narrow isthmus in Central America.

Most historians agree that the name America was written on at least one of Vespucci's documents, but Vespucci did not name the continent or claim that it was named after him. In his publication, he called the new land 'Quarta Orbis Pars' (the Fourth Part of the Earth). Many scholars believe that Vespucci's documents included a secret map that Columbus is reputed to have had in his possession in 1492. In the 1470s a Portuguese merchant ship was inadvertently blown across the ocean to the Caribbean Islands. In trying to make their way back to Portugal these lost mariners charted the coast from Venezuela to Mexico, and reached the part of Central America that is now Panama. It is believed that natives who lived there gave them information about a canoe passage to another ocean only a short distance away.

Columbus related this to the map that existed at the time and concluded that this would allow passage through to India. The explorers believed that this sea passage was at the Cape of Catigara, which we know today as the strait between Singapore and Sumatra. The Malaysian peninsula, also known as Indo-China, was often confused with India and it was this coastline that Columbus thought he was exploring.

Columbus and his navigators established a settlement on Hispaniola in 1492 and during the following thirteen years explored the Caribbean Islands, Central America and the north coast of South America. He was all the while trying to find the Strait of Catigara so that he could sail through to India. Columbus never did land on the soil of North America, and Vespucci would also have been unaware from his own travels that Central America was a narrow isthmus.

The Portuguese authorities had reprimanded Vespucci for releasing a map they considered to be a state secret.[8] Columbus's secret map was possibly the document in question as it may have been included in the items sent to Waldseemüller.

In 1497, another Italian navigator, John Cabot, sailed in an English ship from Bristol and is credited with being the European who discovered the North American continent. Waldseemüller apparently was unaware of this expedition and, as far as it is known, Cabot's maps and records were not published. The Spanish envoy in London, Pedros de Ayala, however, did make a copy of Cabot's map and he notified his government.

In 1498, Cabot and several English ships ventured again to North America and the evidence suggests that they ultimately fell into conflict with the Spanish explorers.[9] Vespucci almost certainly had the opportunity to see a copy of Cabot's map from his 1497 voyage and it is possible that he saw the records of his later voyage.

How could Waldseemüller have known that North and South America are two separate continents connected by a narrow isthmus and that the west coast of North America is mountainous? Vespucci or another source that he relied on probably obtained such information from native peoples who were able to describe the narrow isthmus and the vast ocean on the other side.

It would be another six years before de Balboa would cross the isthmus and be the first European to see the Pacific Ocean, and another twenty years before

Magellan would sail from South America to Asia and confirm Waldseemüller's overall view of the world.

If Vespucci had seen and recorded information from Cabot's maps, Waldseemüller had the benefit of the Cabot survey of parts of the eastern seaboard of the New World without knowing who had charted it. Vespucci's interpretation of any locations named by the English on Cabot's charts would have been transferred to his maps.

Waldseemüller's world map was accompanied by a booklet called the *Cosmographiae Introductio*. It was written in Latin and its main purpose was to explain his work. It is believed that Matthias Ringmann was responsible for the *Cosmographiae*. The booklet included the Introduction, the explanation of the origin of the word 'America', *The Four Voyages of Amerigo Vespucci* as an appendix, and a 'gore', a drawing of the map which can be cut out and assembled into a globe (see page 2).

The following is a translation of Waldseemüller's description of the world:

The purpose of this booklet is to write a description of the world map, which we have designed both as a globe and as a projection. The globe I have designed on a small scale, the map on a larger. As farmers usually mark off and divide their farms by boundary lines, so it has been our endeavour to mark the chief countries of the world by the emblems of their rulers.

COSMOGRAPHIAE

Capadociam/Pamphiliam/Lidiã/Ciliciã/Arme
nias maiorem & minorem. Colchiden/Hircaniam
Hiberiam/Albaniam:& præterea multas quas fin
gillatim enumerare longa mora effet. Ita dicta ab ei
us nominis regina.

Nunc vero & hec partes funt latius luftratæ/&
alia quarta pars per Americũ Vefputium(vt in fe
quentibus audietur)inuenta eft:quã non video cur'
Ame- quis iûre vetet ab Americo inuentore fagacis inge
rico nij viro Amerigen quafi Americi terram/fiue Ame'
ricam dicendam:cum & Europa & Afia a mulieri-
bus fua fortita fint nomina.Eius fitû & gentis mo-
res ex bis binis Americi nauigationibus quę fequũ
tur liquíde intelligi datur.

Hunc in modum terra iam quadripartita cogno
fcitur: & funt tres primæ partes cõtinentes: quarta
eft infula: cum omni quãçş mari circûdata côfpicia
tur. Et licet mare vnũ fit quêadmodum & ipfa teli
lus:multis tamen finibus diftinctum/& innumeris
repletum infulis varia fibi noia affumit:quæ in Cof
Prifcia. mographię tabulis confpiciuntur: & Prifcianus in
tralatione Dionifij talibus enumerat verfibus.
Circuit Oceani gurges tamen vndiçş vaftus
Qui ꝗuis vnus fit/plurima nomina fumit.
Finibus Hefperijs Athlanticus ille vocatur
At Boreę qua gens furit Armiafpa fub armis
Dicit ille piger necnon Satur. idễ mortuus eft alijs;

Waldseemüller's *Cosmographiae*, the document
that accompanies his world map of 1507 and
in which he explains his derivation of the
word America from Amerigo Vespucci.
(*The British Library*)

And to begin with our own continent. In the middle of Europe we have placed the eagles of the Roman Empire and with the key (which is the symbol of the Holy Father), we have enclosed almost the whole of Europe, which acknowledges the Roman Church. The greater part of Africa and a part of Asia we have distinguished by crescents, which are the emblems of the Sultan of Babylonia, the Lord of all Egypt, and of a part of Asia.

The part of Asia called Asia Minor we have surrounded with a saffron-coloured cross joined to a branding iron, which is the symbol of the Sultans of the Turks, who rule Scythia this side of the Imaus, the highest mountains of Asia and Sarmatian Scythia. Asiatic Scythia we have marked by anchors, which are the emblems of the great Tartar Khan.

A red cross symbolizes Prester John (who rules both eastern and southern India and who resides in Biberith).

And finally on the fourth division of the earth, discovered by the kings of Castile and Portugal, we have placed the emblems of those sovereigns.

And what is to be borne in mind, we have marked with crosses shallow places in the sea where shipwreck may be feared. Herewith we close.[10]

Waldseemüller was unable to account for the origin of the name America, but he added text suggesting that it could perhaps have been derived from the first name of the Italian navigator Amerigo Vespucci. The finished map portrayed likenesses of both Ptolemy and Vespucci in honour of these two great world figures.

The following translation is part of the *Cosmographiae* in which the map-makers attempted to justify how the name America must have been derived from Amerigo Vespucci:

> But now these parts (Europe, Africa, and Asia) have been extensively explored, and a fourth part has been discovered by Americus Vespuccius; I do not see what right any one would have to object to calling this part Americus; who discovered it and who is a man of intelligence, and so to name it Amerige that is the land of Americus, or America, since both Europa and Asia got their names from women.[11]

Waldseemüller and his group evidently believed that Vespucci discovered South America. Columbus was given credit for the discovery of the Caribbean, but there is no mention of Cabot and the English voyages. Matthias

Ringmann may have put forward the theory of the origin of the name America, since it was he who wrote this text. Ringmann was only twenty-one years old when the project started; he was young and probably in awe of Vespucci. Waldseemüller's spelling of the name America strongly supports the argument that he saw it in writing.

Spain did not recognize the name for 300 years, but in England it may have been already independently gaining widespread use. Richard Hakluyt, author of *Principall Navigations* published in England in 1589, described the lands as '. . . the fourth part of the world, which more commonly than properly is called America'.[12] By 1538, its use was so prevalent that Mercator used it on his map for both North and South America.

Waldseemüller's world map was published on 27 April 1507 and a second edition followed just four months later. In 1508 Waldseemüller wrote to Ringmann that the map was selling far and wide and he later wrote that over 1,000 prints had been sold. It is likely that by 1508 almost every university, library, and government map room in Europe had a copy. It was well known to historians despite the fact that all the known copies had long since disappeared. The map was unique in more ways than one. It was the first to show the world with the new fourth continent. This new concept of the world fascinated politicians, merchants and adventurers alike. Europeans from several nations were now looking to explore and exploit this new land for its promised wealth.

The map was mass-produced by the new printing press, and its widespread propagation throughout Europe was one of the first consequences of typography. The printing press was embraced by scholars, artists, and businessmen alike to further education, industry, and art, not unlike today's World Wide Web. Up to this time, all maps had been individually drawn. They were expensive, few in number, and not widely seen. This map was being prominently displayed in hundreds of institutions that had not previously possessed a map of any significance. Thousands of people, many of whom had never seen a map before, saw and studied Waldseemüller's map.

A short time after the distribution of the first edition of the 1507 world map, the Duke of Lorraine and the group at St Dié must have received complaints about the prominence of Vespucci's contribution to the map to the almost total exclusion of Columbus's role. Waldseemüller made an attempt to reverse his error. Later editions of the world map dropped the name America and all references to Vespucci.

Father Bartholomeo de Las Casas, Bishop of Chiapaz in Spain, would later write a biography of Columbus. It is very likely, but by no means certain, that he was the main critic. He would later write 'He [Amerigo

Vespucci] is said to have placed the name America in maps, thus sinfully failing towards the Admiral' (1559).[13]

In 1513, Waldseemüller published a seafaring chart of the Caribbean area, including a portion of South America. The name America did not appear at all, and the southern continent that he had previously called America is merely designated as *Terra Incognita*, an unknown territory. He removed all Vespucci's contributions to the 1507 map: all indications of a separate continent, the isthmus, the west coasts of the Americas, the name America, and any reference to

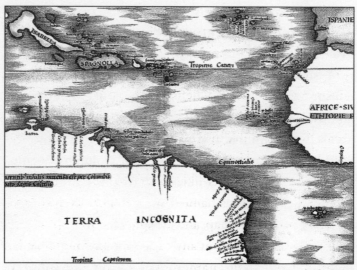

Waldseemüller's World Map of 1513: he has changed the word 'America' (from his 1507 map) to '*Terra Incognita*', thereby crediting Columbus with the discovery of America. (*Bell Library, University of Minnesota*)

Vespucci. Finally, and most significantly, he added a paragraph in which he gave Columbus credit for discovering the New World.

However, it proved impossible to erase the effect of the widespread distribution of the first edition. After its publication, it remained the primary reference map for over twenty years and was copied by several other map-makers. Peter Apian used the name America in exactly the same way in his 1520 world map.

Waldseemüller was unaware of the origin of the name America, a name which clearly pre-dated the period when he drafted the map. The name may have been in use in Bristol in the early 1500s by the seafaring community there. Many Bristol ships had sailed to the fishing grounds of Brassyle by this time. However, the concept of this land being a separate continent was not realized in Bristol until sometime after 1507, perhaps when a copy of Waldseemüller's map arrived in the city. Bristol ships were still searching for a north-west passage through the islands to Cathay.

By the 1530s, it is likely that the southern part of the New World was named America thanks entirely to Waldseemüller's map and the many other published copies. It is possible, in any case, that the northern half would have been named America because of its continuous use by English mariners and merchants for over forty years.

In 1538, Gerard Mercator published his world map in Duisberg, in the Duchy of Cleves. He extended the use of the name America by writing 'North America' and 'South America' on the two parts of the continent, and it has been that way ever since.

Whether or not Waldseemüller can be accused of recklessness for giving credit to Vespucci is a moot point. The map that at this pivotal point in history bade a nebulous goodbye to Ptolemy, heralded Vespucci, and ignored Columbus and Cabot, was thrust into the forefront of academe by means of a modern invention – the printing press.

By the 1830s the name America was fully established but, in the absence of copies of Waldseemüller's map, the derivation of the word remained a mystery.

In the nineteenth century a German explorer and scientist, Alexander von Humboldt (1769–1859), was the first to question how America came by its name. Humboldt published a five-volumed work, the *Cosmos* (1845–62) in which he suggested that America obtained its name by an accident that deprived Columbus of the honour.[14]

Until 1901 it was believed that all the existing copies of Waldseemüller's map had deteriorated beyond recognition or disappeared by the 1600s. However, a single copy surfaced in that year at the family castle of Prince Johannes Waldburg-Wolfegg, at Wurttenberg, in southern Germany.

Johann Schöner (1477–1557), a Nuremberg astronomer and geographer, had acquired this copy when it was first published. Instead of displaying it, as was intended, he bound it into a book along with other maps. (Schöner also produced a globe, which closely duplicates Waldseemüller's gores).

This volume was acquired by the ancestors of Prince Waldburg-Wolfegg after Schöner's death. For nearly 350 years it remained unknown and unread, in the Prince's library collection in the Wolfegg Castle.

In 1901 Joseph Fisher, a Jesuit historian, who was conducting some research in the library of Prince von Waldburg zu Wolfegg-Waldsee discovered Schöner's book and identified its contents.

The United States Library of Congress and others tried to acquire the map at that time. Some 500 copies were made, and the Library purchased one reproduction.

In July 2001 arrangements were completed for the United States Library of Congress to purchase the only known surviving original print of the Waldseemüller world map from the current German Prince. At $10 million it will be the Library's single largest acquisition and it will be put on permanent display in the Thomas Jefferson wing in Washington DC. This map is often called 'America's Birth Certificate', being the first to show the continents of North and South America and use the name America.[15] Remarkably, the map is complete and in pristine condition.

Waldseemüller's maps became obsolete within twenty-five years of their original publication – they were probably discarded or scraped off walls and replaced by newer maps of the day. The map was known to have existed, however. A map-maker named Glareanus wrote in about 1510 that he had worked from Waldseemüller's map, but no one really knew what it looked like.

An intriguing new theory that the name America enjoyed acceptance in England as early as 1500 surfaced around 1900, but much of the twentieth century would elapse before a little-known Welshman, Richard Amerike, would be recognized for the role he played in the naming of America.[16]

T W O

THE COMMERCIAL
REVOLUTION

Spices grow in the lands to the west,
even though we usually say to the east,
for he who sails west will always find
these lands to the west,
he who travels to the east by land
will always find the same lands in the east.

Paolo dal Pozzo Toscanelli (Florence), letter to Canon Fernao
Martinez, Canon of Lisbon cathedral, 25 June 1474.[1]

The Black Death, the flea-borne plague that swept across Europe between 1346 and the early 1400s, exacted a terrible toll. One-third of the population died and economic stagnation lasting a hundred years followed. However, by the mid-1400s, Europe's population was rapidly increasing and an affluent merchant class emerging. This was the beginning of the 'Commercial Revolution'.

Urban centres changed dramatically in Europe at this time. Paris was the largest city with a population of nearly 100,000. It dominated a rural country scattered with smaller urban centres. London was the next biggest city. England was also largely an agricultural nation with many small market and county towns. Paris and London had always been rivals, and the 1400s were a particularly adversarial time.

The third major city in central Europe was the port of Antwerp, situated on the River Schelde, adjacent to the delta of the Rhine, the major artery into the heart of Europe. Along this river flowed virtually all the export trade from Germany, eastern France, Switzerland, and Belgium.

Many English merchant ships plied the waters trading between London and the ports of Calais, Antwerp, Amsterdam, and Bergen, although frequent political problems and changes in customs duties affected this trade. London dominated foreign commerce in England, with 60 per cent of the goods leaving and entering England passing through its port.

Europe saw a tremendous and growing demand for spices, silk, and other exotic goods from the East. In 1271, a young Venetian by the name of Marco Polo set out with his father and uncle on an overland journey through Asia and as far as Cathay, returning a quarter of a century later by sea. During these travels, Polo marvelled at the many spices used both for cooking and medicinal purposes. He wrote of Java, 'from thence also is obtained the greatest part of the spices that are distributed throughout the world'. Polo wrote that the Indian city of Delhi 'produced large quantities of pepper and ginger, with many other articles of

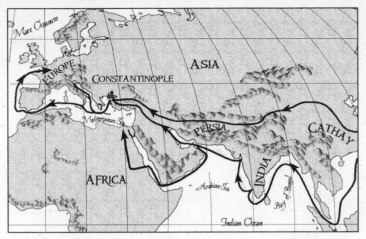

Principal Spice Routes and the Silk Road. (*Courtesy of Jeff Reynolds*)

spicery'.[2] On his return to Venice, he brought with him some of the exotic spices and silk goods he had accumulated during his travels.

From the foundations laid by Marco Polo, by 1450 the Venetians had established a monopoly of the spice trade. These goods travelled overland along the spice routes from Persia to Asia Minor, or by sea from India and Cathay to the Arabian ports and then overland, the routes converging in Constantinople.

The spice trade involved the cooperation of people from different cultures as the goods were sold from merchant to merchant on their journey westwards. At the far eastern end, the Chinese collected cloves and nutmeg from the East Indies and delivered them to the Malaysian port of Malacca. Muslim merchants from

India, Malacca, and Arabia transported them across the Bay of Bengal to India. There, the cinnamon from Ceylon and locally produced pepper were added to the cargo and sold in the spice ports of Calicut, Cochin, Cannore, Goa, and Gujerat along the western coast of India. From India, the goods were sent to Persia, Arabia, and East Africa. Most of the cargo was taken by boat through the Persian Gulf to Shatt-al-Arab. Marco Polo had written of the city of Ormus, situated at the entrance to the Persian Gulf, that it was the 'port frequented by traders from all parts of India who bring spices and drugs . . . These they dispose to a different set of traders, by whom they are dispersed throughout the world.' The goods were then taken by riverboat and camel caravan to Aleppo, Damascus, and eventually Constantinople. Other overland caravans from Cathay through Tibet and Persia also converged on Constantinople.

In Constantinople, Venetian merchants loaded the spices onto their ships, which then sailed to Venice and other Mediterranean ports for distribution into the European market. Just once a year, a convoy of Venetian galleons carried spices through the Mediterranean, out into the Mare Oceanum, and north to England, Holland, and the Baltic region. The profits made by the Venetians were staggering. It was said that if they lost five out of six ships they would still show a profit.[3]

Pepper and ginger from India were particularly in demand. Pepper, the more valuable of the two, was used in cooking and also as a tonic, a stimulant, an insect repellant, and an aphrodisiac. Cinnamon came from Cathay and Burma and was used for cosmetics, drugs, balms, oils, and perfume, all in addition to flavouring food. Nutmeg came from the Banda Islands and cloves from the Moluccas, also known as the Spice Islands.

The affluent used spices extensively for cooking. After the autumn harvest, there was very little fresh food available in Europe until the following spring. In the northern countries, food was not very palatable, particularly in winter. Spices, however, especially pepper, enhanced the taste of meat and other foods. It became a mark of social standing to have these exotic tastes in the food one served, even when the meat was fresh.

But just as European demand for spices burgeoned, in 1453 the supply was suddenly disrupted when the Turks took control of Constantinople. Their victory brought defeat to the Christian Byzantine Empire, and effectively blocked the spice route, diverting traffic south through Alexandria in Egypt. While goods still got through to the markets, transport costs greatly increased and the countries through which the trade now passed exacted high customs duties. The price of Indian pepper increased thirty-fold during the fifteenth century.

It was these economic incentives offered by the spice trade that encouraged Portuguese and Spanish merchants to step up their efforts to find a different route to bring spices to Europe and to enable them to compete with the Venetians. The Portuguese, in particular, believed it would be possible to sail around Africa to reach India by sea. This route, if established, would have the advantage of enabling ships to sail from Asia to Western Europe without having to unload their goods and transport them overland. Merchants could thus import wares unimpeded and duty free.

In 1475, the Italian cosmologist Toscanelli produced a map that offered a totally new concept. He showed that it would be possible to reach India by sailing westwards across the Mare Oceanum. The ports facing that sea on the western edge of Europe would now gain a new significance, one that would not be lost on Christopher Columbus.

THREE

A YOUNG GENOESE ARRIVES IN BRISTOL

To this island [Iceland], which is as big as England, the English merchants go, especially those from Bristol . . . there were vast tides, so great that they rose and fell as much as twenty-six fathoms in depth.

Journals of Christopher Columbus.[1]

In October 1476, Christopher Columbus (or Christoforo Colon), a 26-year-old Genoese seaman, was working on a merchant ship sailing between the English ports of Southampton and Bristol. The ship, along with several other vessels, had rounded the Cornish peninsula and was waiting in the wide estuary of the Bristol Channel for the tide to turn. Two or three hours later, with the incoming tide, the skipper sailed the vessel into the River Avon and moored at the Hungroad. It was a 6-mile trip up the river to the city of Bristol. Several rowing boats, each with six oarsmen and a coxswain, rowed out from the hamlet of Pill to meet the ship. Ropes were thrown down and attached to the rowing boats, which then towed the large ship, guiding it upriver. The swelling tide carried the vessels at a speed faster than a man could walk.

The ships headed up the river in a convoy. After they had been travelling for about 4 miles, they found themselves in a narrow gorge flanked by almost vertical cliffs that towered 300 feet over the river. They passed the Manor of Clifton and the Abbey of St Augustine and then sailed into the very heart of the city itself, a bustling community 10,000 strong. They arrived just before high tide.

The ship was tied up at the quayside and the crew prepared to unload the cargo. Columbus noticed that other ships were getting ready to leave on the outgoing tide. The rowing boats that had piloted the Genoese ship into the centre of the city were now assigned to outgoing vessels. Departing ships were carried along by the current, back through the gorge to the mouth of the river, and out into the Bristol Channel, where the full sails would be raised.[2]

Six hours later, the ships that had remained in the harbour lay stranded on the muddy river bottom. The river had dropped to little more than a stream just a few feet wide. This phenomenon repeated itself twice each day, and it was something Christopher had never witnessed before. He was astonished by tides such as these, where the sea fell 35 feet in just six hours.[3]

It is thought by some scholars that Christopher may have found work in Bristol as an ordinary seaman on a merchant ship going north to the fishing ports of Iceland. There was a small Genoese community settled in Bristol, and he might have been steered to the church of St Nicholas, the patron saint of sailors, and to the Mariners' Institute on Marsh Street. There he would have found out when the ships were sailing and who was hiring.

This theory, that Columbus visited Bristol and sailed to Iceland, most likely on a Bristol merchant ship, is pieced together following the writings of Columbus's son, Fernando Colon, who compiled a book based on his father's notes and recollections, written after his father had died. Fernando described the extreme 50-foot tides that Christopher Columbus could only have observed in Bristol and the nearby River Severn.[4] Fernando transcribed his father's words: 'At the time I was there the sea was not frozen, but there were vast tides, so great that they rose and fell as much as twenty-six fathoms in depth.' Fernando was not familiar with either Bristol or Iceland. The sea does not freeze in Bristol, and there are no extreme tides in Iceland.

Two or three large merchant ships sailed from Bristol to Iceland every year, and Christopher may have been hired to work on a vessel that sailed in February 1477. The Icelandic dried fish trade was originally pioneered and later dominated by the Canynges Company, which earlier in the fifteenth century owned the largest fleet of ships in Bristol.[5] The founder, William Canynges, who had been both Mayor and Member of Parliament for Bristol, died in 1474. By

1477 other merchant companies were occasionally sailing to Iceland.[6]

The ship's cargo contained a variety of utilitarian goods, mostly produced in the west of England. Cheese, butter, honey, and grain were always in demand, and the Bristol ships also supplied metal tools, cheap Flemish linen, and basic commodities, such as vinegar, salt, and wood. Christopher would have noticed the trademarks chalked on the lids of the barrels, identifying the merchants who owned the contents. Typically, three or four merchants would have had cargo on board. The accounts of each merchant were kept separately.[7]

The ship sailed the traditional route: out into the Bristol Channel, heading west along the South Wales coast, and then north into the Irish Sea, following the Welsh coastline and north to the west coast of Scotland. Weather conditions in the Irish Sea could be extremely rough, and a high level of seaworthiness was required of the vessels undertaking these voyages to the edge of the Mare Oceanum and beyond. Trade with Iceland had grown out of the regular Irish trade as early as the 1420s.

They were now out in the open ocean and sailed north across 500 miles of the north Mare Oceanum, passing to the west of the Faeroe Islands at the halfway point. After about twenty days at sea, they reached Iceland.

As they approached the Icelandic shoreline, Christopher would have noticed the wooden racks on the beaches where codfish hung on poles drying in the

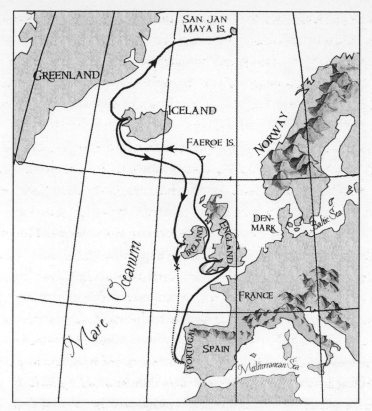

Christopher Columbus's Travels in 1476 and 1477. (*Courtesy of Jeff Reynolds*)

cold air. The racks were called stocks, hence the word 'stockfish'. He was familiar with eating dried salt cod, but this would have been the first time he had seen how it was made. Dried cod was Iceland's major export.

Since Bristol merchants had established trade connections in the Icelandic port of Snaefellsnes, this is most likely where their cargo was unloaded and traded for local goods or cash. The new cargo was then carefully marked with the trademark of its owner.

Fernando said of Iceland, which he referred to as Tile or Thule: 'To this island, which is as big as England, the English merchants go, especially those from Bristol.'[8]

Legally, the ship's purser was not supposed to purchase fish in Iceland. In 1475, in an international dispute with England, Denmark's King Christian decreed that England could no longer buy salt cod or stockfish from Icelandic merchants. The fish was supposed to be purchased in Bergen in Norway where the price could be controlled and taxes collected. Some direct trade was still taking place, but it was severely curtailed. Merchants had begun to search for other fishing grounds.

Columbus's ship may have sailed 400 miles further north to the Arctic Circle, staying within sight of the Greenland coast, and then east to San Jan Maya Island. Fernando's journal includes a detailed description of the distinctive butterfly shape of an island he saw on that trip near the Arctic Circle. That description matches the outline of San Jan Maya Island. Fernando related: 'In February 1477, I sailed myself a hundred leagues beyond Thule whose northern point is seventy-three degrees distant from the equinoctial.'[9]

Ships routinely sailing to Iceland followed the same route every time, returning the same way keeping within the sight of land as much as possible. They would risk leaving the sight of land for a few hours at a time, always watching for the next landmark. It was a particularly cold watch up in the crow's nest, looking for signs of land. Communities would often maintain fires on coastal promontories to assist the seafarers, especially when they relied on them for supplies.

When a ship reached the southern end of the west coast of Scotland, it veered west along the north coast of Ireland, stopping at the port of Galway, a small city on Ireland's west coast with a population of about 4,000. Many Bristol ships, both large and small, sailed to Galway, which had become a primary staging port for many of the ships trading with Iceland, in particular the smaller ones.

Many Portuguese and Spanish ships also sailed to Galway, usually trading wine for fish, supplying the insatiable demand for bacalao, or codfish, in Portugal.

The headquarters for sailors visiting Galway was the church of St Nicholas of Myra, and the Bristol and Portuguese crews visited the church to pray for a safe voyage before they resumed their journeys. Columbus is reputed to have visited this church. In addition to the two references to his visit to England, Fernando Columbus's journal contains a specific reference to Galway. There is a clear implication that Columbus believed that Asia could be reached by sailing west across the ocean. Again, quoting his father, Fernando wrote: 'Men of Cathay, which is toward the Orient, have come hither. We have seen many remarkable things especially in Galway, in Ireland, a man and a woman of most unusual appearance have come to land in two boats.' Two bodies, possibly Eskimos from Greenland, had washed up on the beach, probably in kayaks.[10]

The voyage they had just taken to the north Mare Oceanum was a dangerous one, especially in winter. It would have been cold, wet, and stormy, and Columbus must have wondered to himself why he had left the warm southern climes of his youth. He had firsthand experience with maps and sea charts, but he had stepped out of the confines of the Mediterranean by reaching this far north. The build-up of ice in the rigging made these sailing ships unstable, and a trip of this magnitude involved a high degree of sailing ability and navigational skill.

Columbus most likely returned to Lisbon on one of the Portuguese ships. In Lisbon, he was introduced to the chart-making community, where his talents were soon put to good use.

The young Genoese sailor who had joined the crew in Bristol on the voyage to Iceland in February 1477 was little known at the time. But fifteen years later, he would achieve a position of renown, and then notoriety, and his journals would be preserved for posterity.

BRISTOL SHIPS IN LISBON AND HUELVA

Ships belonging to Bristol in the year of Christ, 1480.
The Mary Grace 300 tons, le . . . of 360 tons, the George 200 tons, Kateryn 180
tons, Mary Byrd 100 tons, Christofer 90 tons, Mary Shernman 54 tons, Leonard
50 tons, the Mary of Bristow . . . le George . . . the John 511 tons, a ship that is
just fitted for sea, John Godeman hath of ships. . . . Thomas Straunge about 12

William Worcestre, Bristol, 1480.[1]

Lisbon had been home to Christopher Columbus for only a few months when he made his trip to England and Iceland. He had arrived there from his native Genoa in the summer of 1476. The son of a middle-class merchant family, Columbus had been at sea since leaving home at the age of fourteen. He sailed the Mediterranean from Spain to Turkey and, with his keen interest in navigation, he sought out the leading cosmographers to learn what he could and hone his skills.

During political upheavals in his home town in 1475, he joined a Genoese merchant ship, one of a convoy of five that was sailing from Genoa to England. A French pirate ship off the coast of Portugal attacked the convoy. The ship that Columbus was on caught fire, and the crew had to abandon ship. Columbus managed to cling to floating debris and swim ashore. He then made his way to Lisbon.

He and the other survivors were soon collected in Lisbon by another Genoese vessel, which had been sent to replace the lost ship. It is thought that this ship may have sailed to London or Southampton and then to Bristol where it spent the winter. This vessel inadvertently introduced Columbus to a city that would play a central role in his career.

Columbus was an ambitious and intelligent young man. He had sailed the full extent of the Mediterranean Sea and, in his early twenties, he wanted to sail the known limits of the seas to increase his knowledge of the world and international trade. His curiosity encouraged him to travel as far north as possible. Sailing to Iceland via Bristol would have afforded Columbus the most reliable and easiest way to sail to the Arctic; Bristol was the only major English port with exposure to the Mare Oceanum.

Whether Columbus visited Bristol in 1476 by accident or by design, the Bristol merchants were the catalyst that inspired him to make his discoveries fifteen years later. Once he had returned to Lisbon in 1477, Bristol ships and their trading routes took on a new significance for him. He was now aware that several Bristol merchants had connections with the Icelandic fish trade. He may also have known some of the merchants themselves.

The *Trinity*, a caravel of 360 tun capacity about 100 feet long, was perhaps the largest ocean-going ship in Bristol at the time. She sailed regularly to Lisbon, southern Spain, and North Africa, while the *Christopher*, a smaller vessel, provided a link between Lisbon, Bristol, and the community of Snaefellnes in Iceland.

By 1478, the *Trinity* had been delivering Bristol's high-quality woollen cloth for fifteen years to the Spanish and Portuguese markets via the ports of Huelva (Seville's ocean port at the mouth of the River Tinto) and Lisbon. The ship usually made the trip twice a year, exchanging its cargo of cloth mostly for wine but also for a variety of foods and general merchandise. Other stop-offs would often be made at Kinsale in Ireland, Santa Maria (the port of Cadiz), Gibraltar, and occasionally Oran on the North African coast.

When the *Trinity* arrived in Lisbon, it would stay in port for three or four weeks. The cargo was unloaded and warehoused, and Lisbon's merchants would barter with the ship's purser for the goods. Many valuable relationships had been established over the years with local businesses. A 'cloth', a bolt of woollen cloth 24 yards long by 3 feet wide, could be traded for about 1 tun of wine, or for as much as 1½ tuns, depending on quality.

Portugal's primary import from Bristol was woollen cloth, but leather goods, manufactured metal goods and glass were also in high demand. Additionally, there

The port of Lisbon, *c.* 1500. (from a contemporary engraving, reproduced in *Voyages Anciens et Modernes* M. Édouard Charton, 1869)

was a market for the barrels of salted codfish or stockfish that Bristol merchants imported from Iceland. Wine was Portugal's major export, reaching up to 200 tuns a month.[2] Olive oil, cork, wax, salt, sugar, fresh fruit, and other foodstuffs were also sold in large quantities. Visits to the port of Lisbon yielded valuable cargoes for the Bristol traders and could be worth more than £1,000 per payload, almost as much as the value of the ship itself. Several English merchants lived in the Portuguese capital and acted as agents for their employers in Bristol. Columbus and his brother probably knew some of them.[3]

The visit to Huelva was even more important to the Bristol merchants than Lisbon, and the *Trinity* would stay there for about a month. According to Castilian or Spanish law, Seville was the major port of entry for most goods imported by sea from Northern Europe into Castile. As in Lisbon, woollen cloth was traded for local produce. The estate of the Duke of Medina Sidonia, the leading Spanish nobleman in Andalucia, was a regular supplier of large quantities of wine to the Bristol market.

During their stay in Huelva, the captain and the crew of the *Trinity* often called at the monastery of Santa Maria at La Rabida. One of the friars, Father Marchena, was an aspiring humanist and an expert in astronomy, astrology and cosmography. He was particularly interested in learning from the English mariners about the voyages to Iceland and the Arctic, and the rumours of islands to the west of Iceland and Greenland. Before leaving port, the captain would settle the account with the prior, Juan Perez, and make a donation to the monastery in exchange for prayers for the safety of the ship and its crew. One such payment is recorded in the accounts of the *Trinity*.[4]

Columbus would have heard of the many legends told about large islands to the west, far out in Mare Oceanum. English ships first journeyed from Bristol to the Faeroes and Iceland in 1424. Icelandic fishermen and adventurers had travelled to Greenland and even further west to other islands. Columbus may even have been aware of the Vinland map, which supposedly was drawn in Iceland around 1440. This map depicted what are now known as Greenland and part of the coast of the Canadian province of Labrador.

In addition to Iceland and Greenland, Columbus would have heard of the Island of Seven Cities and the Island of Brassyle. It was believed that the Island of Seven Cities was located approximately a thousand miles west of Portugal. This island occurs on all Portuguese maps of this period dated later than 1400, which indicates the level of confidence held in its existence. Brassyle, thought to be a thousand miles to the north, sometimes could be seen as a glow in the sky from the west coast of Ireland. Brassyle, also called Hi-Brassyle or Brasil, means in Gaelic the 'Isle of the Blest'. It was reputedly a tranquil place where the departed would spend time between the hardships of earth and heaven. Hi-Brassyle first appeared on the Angelino Dulcert Chart produced in 1325. Originally thought to be about a hundred miles west of Ireland, its suspected location gradually moved further offshore as English ships made periodic attempts to find it, without success.

Several islands beyond Africa in the Mare Oceanum were discovered in the fifteenth century as mariners began to travel further from the sight of land and widen the sphere of exploration. The Canary Islands had been known for 200 years, but Madeira was not discovered until 1419. The Azores were first sighted in 1439, but it was 1452 before all the islands in the group were accounted for. By the 1440s Portuguese ships were visiting the Guinea coast of Africa, and the Cape Verde Islands were discovered. A Portuguese ship would first cross the equator in 1471 and sail around the southern tip of Africa in 1488.

The master mariners of Amerike's day relied on a great deal of personal skill in finding their destinations.[5] With only very few tools to work with, they needed to be able to measure five things accurately to determine where they were in relation to the land. These were the position of north; the speed of the ship; time; the ship's latitude; and the depth of water. They were unable to measure longitude except by estimating distances travelled and by using the various maritime skills and intuition they developed.

To calculate the position of north, the magnetic compass was used. This was usually a crude affair and might be a piece of lodestone resting on a piece of wood or a magnetized needle inside a straw, which was floated in a bucket of water. This compass was fairly accurate in Europe because magnetic north lines up approximately with true north. This, however, is not true in other parts of the world. From North America the compass gives a very distorted 'north' because the pole of magnetic north is far out of line with true north. This is why early maps show the eastern seaboard of North America running almost east to west, rather than south-west to north-east.

The speed of the vessel was measured by tossing a piece of wood overboard at the bow and timing how long it took to get to the stern. This method was later improved upon by adding a long length of rope with knots tied at specific points. The speed was calculated by the number of knots that passed through one's hands in a given time.

An hourglass was essential to measure time. Time was continuously measured, and the hour was logged on a peg-board. The time was compared with the noon readings of the sun and the expected time of sunrise and sunset.

A quadrant was used to measure the line of latitude on which the ship was positioned. It consisted of a heavy metal plate with an attached protractor that was hung in the rigging, with a plumb line hanging down to the deck. The navigator sighted along the protractor's edge at either the sun or the North Star and read the angle.

A plumb line with a heavy lead weight was hung over the bow to constantly monitor the depth of the water when the ship neared the coast. The weight had an indent that allowed the crew to sample the seabed.

The substantial increase in the number and successes of the voyages of exploration in the 1400s was partly due to the introduction of the caravel. The ships that pre-dated the caravel had been adequate for the Mediterranean Sea and European coastal waters

Replica of the *Matthew*. (*Courtesy of the Matthew of Bristol*)

between England, Germany, Holland, Northern France, and Ireland, where they usually sailed in moderate conditions and were seldom out of sight of land.

The caravel was a departure from earlier ship designs, with a high forecastle being added at the bow of the vessel and a similar aft cabin. Usually the sails and rigging consisted of three masts, with the aft mast having a separate near-horizontal pole lashed to it with a triangular lateen sail attached. The other two masts were rigged with a yardarm and standard square sails.

The lateen sail enabled a ship to point about five degrees into the wind, something that had not been possible before. Previously a ship could only make headway if the wind was coming from behind the ship. Consequently sea captains could now take much longer voyages into uncertain waters, leaving the sight of land with the confidence that they would be able to return to their home ports by tacking and sailing slightly into the wind.

It was inevitable that these improvements in ship design would originate in Lisbon, a major port directly exposed to the Mare Oceanum. Small Portuguese ships were soon travelling up and down the coast to Spanish ports and exploring southwards along the African littoral.

FIVE

SHIPSHAPE AND BRISTOL FASHION

Herring of Sligo and salmon of Bann,
Has made in Bristol many a rich man.

Medieval Bristolian proverb.[1]

The Bristol ships that captured Columbus's imagination would have been a prominent feature of the Lisbon waterfront. They were more seaworthy than ships of other nations and integrated many of the latest advances in design. A hundred years earlier Bristol shipbuilders had copied the design features of the Lisbon caravels. They began building larger vessels, which could carry more profitable cargoes. It was because of these dramatic changes in design and construction that trade with Ireland and, later, with Iceland became possible.

The extreme tides in Bristol's harbour contributed to the city's pre-eminence in shipbuilding. Ships tied up at the harbour quays were effectively beached twice a day, often full of cargo, a serious occurrence that put extraordinary stress on the hulls, necessitating stronger structures. The expression 'shipshape and Bristol fashion' originated from this challenge. Care had to be taken when unloading a cargo. The ship could suddenly shift as the tide fell. This could be devastating: shifting cargoes could injure people inside and severely damage the ship. Shipowners favoured one area of Bristol's harbour because the river bottom was muddy, and the hulls could rest easily in the mud.

Tides also meant that dry docks were relatively easy to build in Bristol. A basin was cut into the riverbank and the entrance was secured with a pair of solid wooden gates opening out to the river. The pressure of the high water kept the doors closed, locked against each other. Ships could be dry-docked on every tide. Consequently, ships could be well maintained. A merchant ship had an average seaworthy life of between ten and fifteen years, during which time the ship's carpenter was an essential crew member who would be

Coat of Arms of the City of Bristol. (*Bristol Evening Post Bristol Records Office*)

employed to caulk leaks and replace wood structures, sails, and ropes during most voyages. Maintenance was a continuous process.

Bristol was England's second largest city and one of the world's major seaports. The port of Brygestowe ('bryge' means bridge and 'stowe' is a place of assembly) was established in the tenth century. In the 1080s, soon after the Norman invasion, William the Conqueror authorized the construction of a castle, and the city was granted a seal in 1350. Although devastated by the Black Death, by 1425, then known as Bristowe, the city had expanded and, thanks to its favourable location, had begun to thrive.

Exports from Bristol to Portugal, Spain, Gascony, and Ireland
29 September 1479 to 3 July 1480.[2]

Destination	Sailings	Broadcloths
Portugal	4	441
Spain	8	950
Gascony	7	315
Ireland	31	492
Iceland	2	

Cloth made up 90–5 per cent of exports to Portugal, Spain and Gascony.

Imports to Bristol from Portugal, Spain, and Gascony
29 September 1479 to 3 July 1480.

	Portugal	Spain	Gascony
Wine	206 tuns	197 tuns	816 tuns
Woad	£4	£424	£2,448
Iron		£285	£94
Oil	£923	£169	
Sugar	£426	£100	
Wax	£209	£20	
Soap		£63	
Fruit	£191	£4	
Salt		£83	
Other goods	£87	£114	£31
Total	£1,924		£1,179

£2,573
(excl. wine)

Strategically located between trading centres in Iceland, Spain and Portugal, Bristol offered safe anchorage for its fleet of merchant ships on a protected, easily defensible river. It had developed into a thriving commercial centre serving the west of England, which it remains to this day.

Bristol is surrounded by rich farmland, which supports dairy, arable and sheep farming. Hundreds of small ships delivered wool, hides, and coal from South Wales, iron and oak trees from the Forest of Dean and tin and fish from Devon and Cornwall. The River Severn and its tributaries are major arteries extending into the centre of England, along which ships supplied grain and wool from Gloucester, Worcester, and as far away as Coventry and Ludlow, and the River Wye brought goods from Monmouth, Ross, and Hereford. Extensive cottage industries developed, processing the local agricultural produce and the raw materials arriving by ship.

The city was built within a large bend in the River Avon, which meandered over a flat area of marshland before reaching the gorge. Protected by the river on three sides, a high city wall completed Bristol's defences. The city was contained in an area between St Augustine's Abbey and the Castle and covered little more than a square mile. Ten thousand people worked in the countless small workshops clustered in the narrow streets and alleyways around the older Castle area, across the river in Redcliffe, and along the banks of the river.

The local production of large quantities of high-quality woollen cloth increased dramatically in the early 1400s, when Bristol rose to prominence in the cloth market, a position it retained for 100 years. Edmund Blanket owned one of the largest weaving factories a century earlier. The manufacture of woollen cloth was the major industry, but a number of other, small manufacturing industries had developed. Glass products were made in caves in the red cliffs by St Mary Redcliffe Church. Hides were imported and made into shoes and gloves, and many metal shops manufactured tools, guns, church bells, and hardware. Both coal and lead were mined locally.

The docks constantly bustled with activity, most goods being moved by water even within England. There was constant activity all along the quays as the dock workers unloaded the cargoes and loaded other merchandise on board. Sixteen hundred sailors worked for Bristol shipping companies, and they and the dock workers patronized the numerous taverns on the crowded waterfront. Bristol's skyline was one of rooftops huddling together, smoking chimneys, tall sailing masts along the river, and the towering spires of her many churches. The Church was powerful and supported education and academic life for those who could take advantage of it.

In 1470 the city of Bristol was still small and compact. Most of the city was exactly as shown on Hoefnagle's map published in 1581, and the street plan of the old city centre remains essentially the same today. But the commercial centre, which lay between the Broad Quay and the Back Quay, reflected the wealth of the city's trade and was full of imposing buildings and business properties.

The introduction of the caravel had enhanced Bristol's commercial role and established it as an

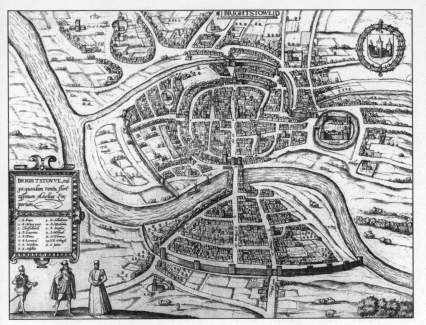

Hoefnagle's 1581 Map of the City of Bristol. (*Bristol Museums & Art Gallery*)

international port. The rapid growth in exports of locally produced goods and the increased imports of Mediterranean foods and wine created not only tremendous wealth and diversity in the city but also a new wealthy class, that of the international merchant trader. It was into this vibrant community that Columbus entered when he arrived in Bristol in 1476.

SIX

The Fellowship of Merchants

At capfinister go your cours north north est,
And ye gesse you ij parties ovir the see
and be bound into sebarne ye must north
and by est till ye come into Sowdying.

Rutters directing a ship from Cape Finistere, Portugal,
to the Severn estuary and on to the shallow water (soundings) near
Bristol.[1]

Sturmy's House, a former private residence, was located on the quay by Bristol Bridge near the church of St Nicholas. Robert Sturmy, a wealthy merchant, had given the property to the city to be used as the Cloth Hall, the exchange where woollen cloth makers sold their cloth for shipment overseas. A portion of the building was used as the meeting place of an organization known as the Fellowship of Merchants.

The Fellowship of Merchants was founded in 1467 by Bristol's wealthiest and most politically powerful merchant traders. Their goal was to organize trade and the local shipping industry to their own advantage. Little is known about this organization but it is recorded that they met to fix the prices charged to non-

Bristol Bridge, much as it would have appeared in 1500. (*Bristol Evening Post*)

Bristol merchants for various commodities, including wool, wax and oils. Bristol merchants pioneered the formation of business partnerships to finance the construction and ownership of ships, and some have speculated that the Fellowship was instrumental in arranging these ventures and generally in looking after the collective interests of its members. Through their membership, they had important connections with the English government and the King. The Fellowship had close links with the Bristol authorities: the Mayor and City Councillors made all appointments.[2]

Many ships were still owned by individual merchants in the traditional way. The Fellowship, however, may have been the catalyst that enabled several merchants and investors to band together to build and operate a merchant vessel. Much larger ships could be built when the financial risk was spread over several partners.

Thus a new business class evolved – that of the shipowner. These shipowners solely operated ships and assessed freight charges or leased vessels or cargo space to merchants. The ship came complete with a captain and a crew, and generally plied the same route on a regular basis. The profits were such that a caravel could be paid for in just four voyages. Merchant trading companies had only the responsibility of assembling cargoes and trading them in foreign ports.

The *Trinity*, the magnificent 360-tun caravel that regularly sailed to Spain and Portugal, was built in 1463. It had cost about £1,200 to build and was one of the finest ships in England. It was built by a partnership of eight Bristol merchants that included John Jay, John Shipward, William Bridde, Gilbert Smyth and William Wodyngton.[3]

Jay (John Jay I) was the sole owner of several ships and had business interests in many others. In 1477, he placed five ships at the disposal of King Edward IV, and as compensation for this act he was allowed to import goods to the value of £190, duty free. The shares of ownership in a vessel were readily transferable, and on John Jay's death in 1468, his shares passed to his sons, John Jay II and Henry.

In one of its earlier voyages, the *Trinity* delivered 700 cloths to Spain and Portugal, the equivalent of 3 miles of cloth 3 feet wide. This was an enormous cargo for a ship at that time. As many as a hundred different merchants consigned cargo on each voyage, the accounts for each merchant being kept separately by the ship's purser.

Columbus may have known the *Trinity*. It would have been a familiar sight in Lisbon Harbour in the late 1470s. It had a crew of thirty men, and their pay was typically 12*d* a week. The operating costs for the ship were about £8 a week.

The resident purser in the late 1470s was a man named John Balsall, whose trading records for two of the *Trinity*'s voyages were discovered in London just forty years ago.[4]

Many names listed on the bills of lading are familiar to scholars of Bristol's history. John Jay III, William Bird, Robert Straunge, John Esterfeld, William Wodyngton, and Richard Amerike were just a few of the merchants who owned the cargoes of woollen cloth on board. According to the Balsall records, a few women merchants also shipped cloth on the ship.[5]

Two of the names in these trading records would soon appear in an English Crown exploration charter, and many appear on the list of Bristol's Mayors and Sheriffs: Messrs Spencer, Pynke, Esterfield, Straunge, Thorne, and Amerike all served as Mayor or Sheriff of Bristol.[6]

By Balsall's accounts, the *Trinity* returned to Bristol six months later, laden with 76 tuns of wine, 182 tuns of olive oil, 53 cwt of sugar, 59 cwt of wax, and other produce. Richard Amerike was the importer of sugar and olive oil.[7]

Thomas Croft was a business associate of John Jay II. He also held a one-eighth share in the *Trinity*, as well as shares in other vessels. In the late 1470s he was working as the King's Customs Officer in Bristol. This was an honorary appointment, and it was his responsibility to collect all customs duties for the Crown. Croft came from an influential family and had been a friend of King Edward since his childhood at Croft Castle, near Leominster in Herefordshire. The King was raised at nearby Ludlow Castle, and the families were close both socially and politically.

Customs duties were used partly to finance the navy. Piracy had been a major problem in the early 1400s, and for protection merchant ships travelled in convoys, accompanied by one or two navy vessels.

A Bristol merchant starting to rise to prominence, a generation younger than John Jay II, was a man named Richard Amerike. He was a wealthy landowner and merchant trader who, by 1478, was building a successful business trading with merchants in Spain and Portugal. He had built up a trade in exporting high-quality woollen cloth.[8] Only about forty years old, Amerike was a contemporary of John Jay III and, like him, probably ran his family's business. Given the connection between these influential families, it is possible that Amerike or his family also owned a share of the *Trinity*.

Amerike lived with his wife, Lucy, and their two teenage daughters in the Clifton Manor, one-third of which he purchased in 1470 from Sir John Chideock.[9] Amerike's land consisted of about 100 acres of Clifton wood and the adjacent farmland centred around St Andrew's Church and Clifton Green. It included a manor house, many dwellings, and several small tenant farms. The property was situated at the top of a steep hill overlooking the river and the lands of St Augustine's Abbey. Nearby were the cliffs and the steep gorge through which trading ships sailed to reach the city's port.

Amerike's family was almost certainly of Welsh aristocratic descent.[10] His coat of arms provides a common thread that links him to the Welsh rulers of North Wales and Anglesey.[11] Members of this family had been wealthy landowners in the Welsh border country near Ross-on-Wye in Monmouthshire for many centuries. The anglicizing of his surname from Ap Meric to Amerike was still not fully established,[12] and might indicate that the family's move to England was very recent or that the family was resident in Bristol but still had an estate in Wales. Perhaps Amerike's father or grandfather moved to Bristol in the early

1400s to trade wool, which was regularly shipped from Wales to be made into cloth in the Bristol workshops.

Richard Amerike was also a contemporary of Thomas Croft, who was raised on his family's estate in Herefordshire, just a short distance north of Ross-on-Wye. If, indeed, Richard Amerike was born in Ross-on-Wye they may have known each other since childhood.

Richard Amerike was one of about 250 individuals living in Bristol who were trading internationally in the late 1470s. These were not all full-time merchants, but there was a group of about thirty-five wealthy men whose main business was exporting, trading, importing, and distributing foreign goods, investing at least £100 per voyage.

Although the Spanish and Portuguese trade in which Amerike was becoming a dominant figure had only existed for a little over a decade, it was growing rapidly. Prior to 1455, few English ships had ventured further south than the French city of Bordeaux in Gascony. Bordeaux, like much of France, had been an English possession and was the principal source of wine. In 1453, the French re-established control of most of France, and trade with Bordeaux abruptly ceased.

This event exacerbated the Wars of the Roses, which pitted the House of York against the House of Lancaster for control of the English Crown. The

Yorkists were in the ascendancy at the time when the Amerike family's wine trade was interrupted, and the merchant ships were forced to venture into the Bay of Biscay. An uneasy and fragile peace with France was arranged but did little to quell the violent English civil conflict that resulted, and which flared up periodically for more than thirty years.

Richard Amerike's family had been prominent merchants in the Bordeaux trade. An early record shows John ap Meric and Richard ap Meric importing wine on a ship called the *George* in 1436, and Richard Ameryk importing 20 tuns of iron from Spain on the *Valantyn* in 1437. Richard ap Meric/Ameryk may have been Richard Amerike's father.[13]

With the collapse of the wine trade from France, new sources of trade had urgently to be found. Improvements in the design of ships built in the Bristol shipyards enabled the merchant seamen to give Gascony a wide berth and sail further south and across the notoriously rough seas of the Bay of Biscay to Spain and Portugal. By 1479 trade with these countries had grown to over half the value of all foreign trade in Bristol.

In the three months between February and April 1480 Richard Amerike shipped out 12 cloths on the *Mari Birde* to Bordeaux, 5 tuns of corrupt wine and 2 tuns of salt on the *Trinite* to Ireland, and 20 cloths on the *Kateryn* to Lisbon. There exists no record of what these goods were traded for, but the *Kateryn* would have returned to Bristol with at least 5,000 gallons of wine, or the equivalent, in the account of Amerike. In this same period he imported a large shipment of fish and animal hides from Ireland on the *Christopher* of Newport, 3 tuns of olive oil and 2 cwt of sugar on the *Trinite* from Lisbon, and a large quantity of woad from Bordeaux on the *George* of Bristol.[14]

With as many as several dozen individual merchants each owning cargo on any particular voyage, a method was devised to enable the purser to keep track of each merchant's property. Merchants had trademarks that were used to identify their cargoes. This mark was chalked onto the barrels or cargo. Each was distinctive in appearance and was recognized by the Fellowship of Merchants. This same mark was engraved on a ring and used to seal documents with a wax seal.

The ship's purser was often authorized by the shipper to trade his cargo in foreign ports. His sole judgement was relied upon to barter a merchant's cargo for local goods if the merchant did not have a local representative, which was usually the case. The trademarks were an effective way of identifying the cargo when ships were being loaded and unloaded and when the purser was trading.

Most merchants confined their trading to specific geographic areas. There was a growing and increasingly affluent group that traded more or less exclusively with Spain and Portugal. This group bought large

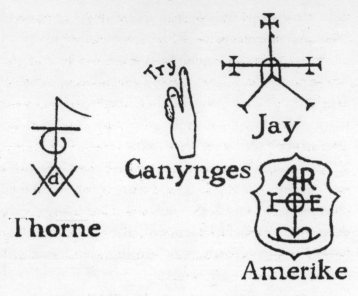

Trade Marks for Thorne, Canynges, Jay and Amerike.
(E.D. Hudd, *Bristol Merchant Marks*)

quantities of woollen cloth for export, confident that they had a market for it.

Another distinct group concentrated on the northern countries of Iceland, the Baltic region, and Ireland. The commodities traded were quite different. Many were fish merchants, and most cargoes were of considerably less value than the cargoes originating from Spain and Portugal.

One of the most important functions of the ship-owners' association was to maintain a Map Room. Before the advent of the printing press, the only charts available were hand drawn. A chart maker in Bristol drew these maps and constantly kept them up to date. They were maintained and kept in a secure place.

Ship captains on English vessels did not have charts but were supplied with 'rutters', which described their assigned voyages. Rutters were small pocket-sized books, handwritten, and providing navigational information. They were kept in the captain's pocket at all times. But the captain did not have the luxury of a dry cabin to work from and was usually on deck, directly exposed to the weather. Other pertinent documents relating to the cargo and the ship, including bills of lading, were taken on board in a leather satchel and stored in a safe, dry place.

When the captain returned to Bristol, any new information he could add was given to the chart maker in the Map Room. If a new island or destination was discovered, rutters would be written or amended and made available for future voyages.

Seamen have always had local names for landmarks and headlands they looked for as the ship approached land. Place-names often grew up in uncharted and obscure ways, recalling, for example, a particular geographical feature or something familiar, a family name, a business or a profession. New names quickly took root through repeated oral usage, and these verbal christenings had justifiable staying power. Names such as Table Mountain, Cape Cod, and Steep Holm originated from informal usage.

Discoverers and explorers, by contrast, often named landmarks after dignitaries or members of the ship's crew, in a more formal process. The captain of the ship entered these names into his charts and there they remained. Captain George Vancouver named most of the landmarks in Puget Sound and around Vancouver Island after English royalty, naval dignitaries and his ship's officers. Puget Sound was named after Peter Puget, one of his officers; Mt Rainier after the admiral; Mt Baker after a junior officer; and, of course, Vancouver Island was named after himself.

It was against this backdrop that the merchants of Bristol were poised to face west when the focus for new fishing grounds demanded attention.

SEVEN

FISH STORY

The sea is swarming with fish, which can be taken not only with the net, but in baskets let down with a stone . . . his companions say that they could bring so many fish that this kingdom would have no further need of Iceland, from which place there comes a great quantity of stock-fish.

Raimondo di Soncino, Milanese Ambassador to London, 1496.[1]

There was a staggering demand for fish throughout Europe in the 1400s. For those who lived on the coast, fresh fish was usually available. However, for people who lived inland, especially in hot climates, the supply of fresh fish was unreliable, expensive or non-existent. Members of the Catholic Church created a demand for fish on Fridays and all holy days, not only in England, but throughout Christendom; and especially in Spain and Portugal.[2]

Norwegian fishermen used an effective process for drying and preserving fish. They exported the process to the Icelandic people and settlers in Greenland. They originally produced stockfish and salt cod for their own consumption, catching the fish and curing it for use when bad weather made fishing impossible. This method was later used to meet the demand for export. The process works best with cod because cod has a

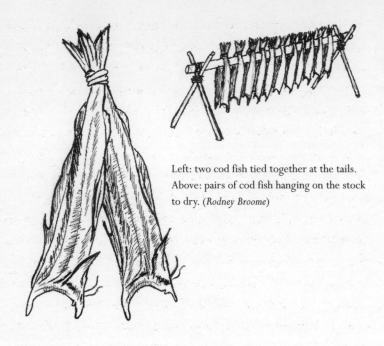

Left: two cod fish tied together at the tails.
Above: pairs of cod fish hanging on the stock
to dry. (*Rodney Broome*)

longer shelf-life than other salted fish, and it rehydrates
and tastes better when reconstituted. For the poor, this
dried fish provided a cheap form of nutrition that
could be stored for long periods.[3]

Fishermen started the process for preparing
stockfish immediately after the catch. The fish were
gutted and the heads removed. They were then filleted,
leaving the two halves joined at the tail, or two or
more smaller fish were tied at their tails so that they
could be hung over poles and placed on stocks, which
the fishermen had built on the beaches. The fish were
effectively freeze-dried in the cold, dry air for six to

eight weeks, during which time they would shrink to a fraction of their original thickness and lose 80 per cent of their weight. The quality of the fish varied depending on the weather and the time of year the fish were dried. When completely dry, the fish were carried loose in boxes or tightly packed into barrels between layers of salt.[4]

Salt cod was made by compressing fresh fillets of cod between layers of salt in barrels. Both types of preserved fish kept for long periods of time, and large quantities of fish could be transported to hot climates without spoiling.

When stockfish was brought to market, it was soaked in a bath of water for many hours. The water was refreshed several times to eliminate most of the salt. As the fish absorbed the water, it swelled, slowly reverting to its original thickness. The fish was then poached and cooked in sauce. It was a tasty and popular food.

Stockfish is produced in Norway and Iceland today, and there is still a thriving export market. The Spaniards have a dish called *baccala*. In Portugal this same dish is called *bacalao*; both are prepared in the same way.

In the first half of the fifteenth century, the Danish–Norwegian authorities increased their regulation of the stockfish market, insisting that shipping pass through the Norwegian city of Bergen, where prices and taxes were controlled.[5] But enforcement of the regulations was lax and a few Bristol ships still traded with Icelandic, and occasionally, Greenland settlements. As the English merchants paid up to twice as much for the fish as their Norwegian counterparts, they were welcome in the small coastal settlements. Most of the larger 200-tun ships sailed north through the Irish Sea between Wales and Ireland, but some would sail into the Mare Oceanum putting into Irish ports, such as Galway. There were also many smaller coastal traders, or doggers, of about a 50-tun capacity, that plied this route with lower value cargoes, such as wood, which they traded for fish.

The *Antony* made a typical voyage to Iceland in 1471:

The ship called the Antony of Bristol in which John Deanfitz is master came from Island on this day (September 10) and has in it for John Forster, denizen, xxxv last lying, value lxx pounds, subsidy lxx shillings for the same, xv last stockfysshe, value lxxv pounds, subsidy lxvv shillings for John Gregorie, denizen, j last salt fish, value x pounds, subsidy x shillings.[6]

A last was a unit of measurement, 640 gallons or the volume of a box 4 feet square and 4 feet deep. The value of this cargo was as follows: thirty-five lasts (probably of fish soaked in lye, or lutefisk): £70; fifteen lasts of stockfish: £75; and one last of salt cod: £10. On each, a subsidy, or duty, was payable of one shilling in the pound, or 5 per cent. A typical value for a cargo in this market was £155. By contrast, the value of a cargo on one of the larger ships from Lisbon or Spain was at least £1,000.

The major commodity needed to make stockfish was salt. The Portuguese had this in abundance, and they also had a huge market for stockfish. But as Bristol merchants had the seagoing ships for these seas, they established a regular trade route in the mid-1400s. Bristol ships returned from Portugal in the spring loaded with salt. Salt was then shipped to Iceland to be traded for stockfish. The ships returned directly to Bristol or sometimes stopped in Galway, where the fish was unloaded and shipped to Portugal and Spain.

With few exceptions, the ships trading from Bristol in the Icelandic and Baltic markets did not usually venture into the Spanish or Portuguese market. An exception was William de la Fount who was involved in trade in Iceland as well as in Spain and Portugal. He was well positioned to supply stockfish and salt cod to the Spanish and Portuguese markets from his own suppliers in Iceland.[7]

A small Icelandic community lived in Bristol. Its members mostly worked for the wealthy merchants as household servants. One Icelandic national living in

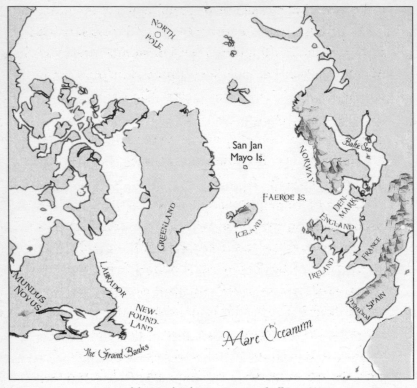

Map of the North Atlantic. (*Courtesy of Jeff Reynolds*)

Bristol was a man named Willelmus Islond. He became a merchant and later specialized in the Portuguese market. He eventually became an English subject.

The Icelandic people have a rich history and folklore of early exploration in the Arctic region. The major fishing grounds are to the south of Iceland, but Icelandic fishermen are known to have ranged as far west as Greenland and Labrador in their search for fish and timber. They established several new communities in the process. In the tenth century, Leif Eriksson sailed from Iceland and founded a settlement at L'Anse aux Meadows, near the northern tip of Newfoundland, which survived for twenty years. The winters were inhospitable, making it difficult to establish a permanent settlement, and it eventually fell into disuse. However, the fishing was better than anyone had ever imagined.

The cold Labrador current flowed south from the Arctic carrying krill, a minute shrimp on which fish fed. The current met the warm Gulf Stream flowing north-east up the eastern seaboard off the coast of Newfoundland on a shallow area we now call the Grand Banks. This cauldron of cold Arctic water and plankton-rich warm water provided a seemingly inexhaustible feed for fish. The St Lawrence River also joins the ocean in this area. These physical features in combination produced what was probably the best fishing area in the world. In July, smelt proliferated and their presence attracted codfish and whales. The cod grew up to 6 feet long and weighed 200 pounds.

Shipping in the entire Baltic region was controlled by an international organization called the Hanseatic League. The League had been formed in Germany in the thirteenth century to regulate trade and control the mouths of the major rivers in Northern Europe. It was initially seen as a positive force, but it gradually came to be dominated by Scandinavian and Northern European interests. The League regulated the fishing industry and gave licences for the exclusive rights to sell fish in specific markets.

A severe blow to English merchants came in 1450, when King Christian of Denmark, the head of the Hanseatic League, banned them from trading while issuing licences of exemption to specific merchants: Bristol's Canynges Company, for instance, was permitted to continue importing fish from Iceland to England.[8] Then, in 1475, the Hanseatic League, at the instigation of the Danish–Norwegian Crown, attempted to monopolize the dried cod trade by completely eliminating the English from the market. To this effect they passed decrees prohibiting English merchants from buying salt cod in Iceland.

Although the impact was dramatic on the economies of both Iceland and Bristol, trade with Iceland did not cease entirely after 1475 – there is a record of two voyages from Bristol to Iceland in 1480, and there were several hostile incidents as a few English ships attempted to circumvent the ban and Danish authorities seized some of the ships. The loss of the Icelandic trade had a devastating effect on the financial fortunes of some of the Bristol merchants involved and it also created a problem for those who specialized in trading in the southern markets. Their customers and agents in Lisbon and

Seville had relied upon them to supply the demand for salt cod.

As Bristol merchants sought new sources of fish, interest began to centre on the mysterious Island of Brassyle, which was thought to lie west of Ireland. Bristol ships travelling to the west coast of Ireland made forays into the Mare Oceanum but had not been able to locate Brassyle. The distance from the Irish coast was thought to be at least 400 miles.

The Icelandic people living in Bristol would have related stories about the known lands to the west beyond Iceland and Greenland where exceptionally good fishing grounds were reported to exist. Willelmus Islond would have been familiar with the stories. The merchants wondered if the place they called Brassyle was the same the Icelanders were describing. William de la Fount, William Spencer, and Richard Amerike each employed Icelandic servants who would have been familiar with Icelandic folklore and legends pertaining to these lands.[9]

De la Fount was the half-owner of the *Christopher*, which often sailed from Bristol to Lisbon and Iceland. One of his skippers, an accomplished seaman by the name of Thomas Sutton, is on record as travelling from Gibraltar to Iceland and back, always passing through Bristol. On a typical voyage he would bring fruit, oil, and salt from Lisbon to Bristol, where only the fruit and oil would be unloaded. The salt and additional cargo would then be sent on to Iceland. On the return haul, some of the stockfish might stay on board in Bristol to be sent south. The ban on fish sales in 1475 must have disrupted de la Fount's business.

Bristol merchants paid special deference to rumours that the Basques in northern Spain had discovered the Island of Brassyle. The Basques' commercial sphere of influence was in the area centred on the port of Bayonne, in the Bay of Biscay. In the mid-1400s, Basque fishermen dramatically increased their fishing catches, and their neighbours to the north, the Bretons, began to notice their increased wealth. Other fishermen began to wonder why the Basques were so successful and where they were catching fish. The Basques refused to reveal the location of their fishing grounds, but it was becoming increasingly more difficult for them to protect their secret.[10]

The Bretons, who traditionally fished out of Brittany, tried to follow the Basques but were unsuccessful. However, their stories of an island across the Mare Oceanum persisted, and seamen from Bristol heard the rumours in the taverns and foreign ports. Denmark's prohibitive decree of 1475 encouraged the Bristol merchants to make a concerted effort to explore and find Brassyle and, perhaps, even the Island of Seven Cities, another Celtic legendary island.

EIGHT

THE SEARCH FOR BRASSYLE

Licence for Thomas Croft and for William Spencer, Robert Straunge and William
de la Fount, merchants of Bristol, to trade for three years to any parts with any
except staple goods, despite any statute to the contrary, with two or three ships,
each of 60 tuns or less.

Licence issued by Edward IV, King of England, 18 June 1480.[1]

The merchants who traded with Spain and Portugal
were those most concerned with the loss of the
salt cod and stockfish trade. The resale of Icelandic cod
to the rapidly growing Spanish and Portuguese market
had been more rewarding financially than sale to the
English market, which was largely satisfied by
imported fish from Ireland.

A few Bristol merchants had long been familiar with
the Greenland coast. Dr Ruddock has speculated that
by 1479 a Bristol ship might have already reconnoitred
a route from Iceland west and south around Greenland
to Labrador or Newfoundland.[2] Whether or not this
theory can be confirmed, it appears that the merchants
had sufficient knowledge of these distant waters to
approach the Crown for an official exploration permit:
in 1479, a delegation of the four most senior and
influential merchants in the Fellowship applied to King

Edward IV for a trading licence to explore and trade in new territories. To this effect, the King granted a trading licence on 18 June 1480 to Thomas Croft, Robert Straunge, William Spencer, and William de la Fount. It restricted the exploration to three ships, each with a maximum cargo capacity of 60 tuns. This meant that they could take three caravels, each about 70 feet long. They were authorized 'to trade for three years to any parts with any except staple goods'. It was further stipulated that the Crown was to receive one-fifth of the profits after all costs had been met.

This licence gave the merchants the backing of the English Crown to explore and trade in new areas and receive the protection of the English government. Foreign governments recognized these documents and diplomats were made aware of the expedition.

The government official and the three merchants named on the document were prominent in Bristol civic affairs, and each owned ships or had businesses trading with Spain and Portugal.[3]

Robert Straunge, aged forty-two and the youngest of the four, was an established wine merchant from a family that owned at least twelve large ships. He had been Mayor of Bristol in 1475 and would be again in 1482 and 1489. He also served two terms as Bristol's Member of Parliament.

William Spencer, aged fifty-seven, was the out-going Mayor. He was later appointed three more times in this capacity and also as Bristol's Member of Parliament. Spencer was the merchant who, with John Pynke, a former Mayor, consigned goods from Lisbon to Bristol on the *Christopher*.[4]

William de la Fount was a wealthy merchant who owned a large 201-tun ship and was also half-owner of the *Christopher*. Thomas Croft was the Customs Officer. He was the owner of a one-eighth share in the *Trinity* with John Jay. In his post as the King's Customs Officer, Croft was

Mayor William Spencer handing over to his successor, Edmund Westcott in 1479. From Robert Ricart's *Kalendar of Bristol*. (*Bristol Record Office*)

responsible for collecting any monies due to the Crown as a result of this trade but, while he could legally own a share of the vessel, he was prohibited from trading himself.[5] Finally, two others, younger men actively involved in business dealings with these merchants, John Jay III and Richard Amerike, may have been junior members of this group.

Meanwhile, regular trade to Spain, Portugal and Ireland continued unabated, and the *Trinity* set sail from Bristol to Lisbon in October 1479 with a full load of woollen cloth. During the winter, several other ships were loaded with similar cargoes bound for the Spanish and Portuguese markets. The outbound ships included the *George* and probably the *Christopher*. They sometimes travelled together for mutual protection.

The *Trinity* arrived back in Bristol on 4 March 1480, fully laden with cargo, including sugar and olive oil, belonging to Richard Amerike. During March and April the ship was unloaded and then restocked with another cargo of cloth. It left Bristol in May 1480 for a similar trip to Lisbon. It eventually returned to Bristol about four months later. Mystery and intrigue still surround the events of this voyage.

One of the ship captains employed by Jay was a man named Lloyd. If indeed he was the skipper on this particular voyage, then the return trip to Bristol was not straightforward. The *Trinity* left Lisbon on 15 July 1480, and seemingly took a clandestine detour to look for a mysterious island in the Atlantic. According to William Worcestre:

[Bristol men] in two ships of 80 tuns, of Jay, junr [John Jay III]. A merchant, who began their voyage 15 July 1480, at the port of Bristol at Kynroad, for the island of Brasyle, taking their course from the west part of Ireland, plowing the seas through, and Thlyde (Lloyd) is master of the ship, the most skilful mariner in all England. . . . News came to Bristol Monday 18th September, that the ships sailed over the seas for nine months, and found not the island, but through tempests at sea returned to port in Ireland, for laying up their ships and mariners.[6]

Worcestre was a prolific writer who documented much of Bristol's history during his day. He was the brother-in-law of John Jay II; John Jay III was his nephew. The voyage he described may have left Lisbon (rather than Bristol) just four weeks after the licence had become effective.

Worcestre's writings describe two 80-tun ships that belonged to John Jay and that sailed from Bristol with Lloyd, 'the most skilful mariner in England', as Master in overall charge. They were trying to find the Island of Brassyle, which was believed by now to be about 400 miles to the west of Ireland. After searching the Mare Oceanum for nine weeks, the ships did not return to Bristol but put into a port in Ireland, from where news reached Bristol via another ship. The transcript of a trial the following year raised the possibility that one of these ships may have been called the *Trinity*.

Worcestre was quite old when he wrote this account and was living in Norfolk. In writing his family's journals, he probably used letters and stories he received from members of his family. He obviously erred when he described the voyage as being nine months instead of nine weeks, and he may have confused the date the ship left Lisbon with the date he thought it left Bristol. Worcestre's writings were a private journal but if the Jays were using the large 360-tun *Trinity* instead of a smaller 60-tun vessel allowed by the trading licence, they may have purposely misled him. Whether or not the *Trinity* ships named were one and the same vessel or different ones, they did share common ownership by the Jay family.[7]

In October 1480 the larger *Trinity* was back in Bristol and set sail that month under the command of Master Rychard Parker for another uneventful voyage to southern Spain with a cargo of 400 bolts of woollen cloth. The young merchant Richard Amerike owned a portion of this shipment. It followed its regular trading route from Bristol to the Welsh port of Pembroke. From there, it sailed to Kinsale in Ireland and then with a full cargo to Huelva in Spain. It stayed in Huelva for a month and while there John Balsall, the purser, traded much of the cargo for cash and goods. His accounts recorded in detail the sales he made of goods unloaded in Huelva, Castile, on 27 November 1480:

In primus y recevid by the grace of God out of the *Trynety* by ffore wreten at Welva ffor the name of Master Wylliam Spencer marchaunt of Brystowe . . . conteyneng vii holl cloths . . . 7 holl cloths
Item . . . Master Straynge . . . 5 holl cloths
Item . . . Master Esterfyld . . . 7 holl cloths

Item . . . Master Edmond Wescott . . . 5 holl cloths

Item . . . Master William Bryd & John Jay . . . 11 holl cloths

Item more y recevid of the seyd schep at Welva yn the name of Rychard Amyreke

marchaunt v holl cloths under the mark made in the margent — v (5) holl cloths.[8]

The group of six merchants Balsall refers to includes the same William Spencer and Robert Straunge who had recently been granted the licence to trade and also two younger merchants named John Jay and Richard Amerike. Amerike is listed last and is the only one of the group that Balsall does not defer to as 'Master'.

The ship then sailed further south, stopping in Gibraltar, and into the Mediterranean Sea to Oran in North Africa. On the return trip, in April 1481, the *Trinity* again stopped in Huelva, trading more cargo for wine and oranges before returning to Bristol. Cargo was traded at every port to maximize profits.

No official records exist stating how many exploratory voyages the Bristol merchants made either that summer or in the following two years in their search for new fishing grounds, or of their luck. The merchants had little to gain if word got out that they were successful. Their only concern was to find markets to trade in and import fish. Had it not been for Worcestre's personal writings documenting the dealings of his relatives, the Jay family, we would not know of any voyages made in the first year under the trading licence.

In October 1480 there was another voyage. One of the ships called *Trinity* set sail from Bristol. The destination was recorded as Ireland. Richard Amerike consigned on board a cargo of 2 tuns of salt and 6 tuns of corrupt wine. Ian Wilson, in his book *The Columbus Myth* proposes that this cargo was destined to be shipped across the Mare Oceanum to Brassyle and that Ireland was not the intended destination. Salt would have to be imported to Bristol, most of it from Portugal. Consequently, it was fairly expensive. This was a significant investment for Amerike and one that would require appropriate arrangements be made at the receiving end.

The following summer, in July 1481, the *Trinity* and another ship called the *George* were both in Bristol, and they were again loaded with salt and other supplies. Thomas Croft and John Jay owned shares in these ships. The destination for these ships was also recorded as Ireland, but this proved not to be entirely true. The journey, which should have taken three weeks, took nearly three months.

These trading voyages were supposed to show a profit, and if the merchants were bringing fish back to Bristol, there were no records of any fish imports in Croft's customs accounts.

According to the terms of the licence, the merchants should pay 20 per cent duty on imported goods resulting from trade, after all costs were subtracted.

There may have been other forays in the three years following the summer of 1480. Perhaps a ship from Bristol found Brassyle along with fishing camps that had been set up there by the Basques. If this is the case, the Bristol ship was there only to trade. The terms of their licence did not give them any jurisdiction to claim the land for England.

On the other hand, if they had established a fishing settlement and were catching the fish themselves, the fish would not have been acquired by trade and would therefore not be taxable. This, and the movement of large quantities of salt and corrupt wine, support the idea that Jay, Croft, and perhaps Amerike, had indeed established their own fishing settlement. These events did not go unnoticed in London.

Immediately after the *Trinity* and *George* returned to Bristol, suspicions were roused and questions asked in London about the real purpose of the voyage. The government evidently believed that Croft and the Bristol merchants were trading and illegally importing goods, thus evading the 20 per cent payment to the Crown. A Royal Commission was sent from London in September to examine their activities. In October 1481, Thomas Croft, the Customs Agent, was arrested and charged with engaging in foreign trade:

Croft Coat of Arms and trade marks of Robert Straunge and William Spencer.

Thomas Croft of Bristol. . . . Customer of the said lord the king in the port of his town of Bristol aforesaid on the sixth day of July in the aforesaid year [1481] . . . was owner of an eighth part of a certain ship or balinger called the Trinity, and an eighth part of a certain ship or balinger called the George, and in each of the said ships or balingers . . . laded, shipped and placed forty bushels of salt . . . with the intention of trading.[9]

Croft pleaded that the *Trinity* was exploring rather than trading. He said in his defence that he was only trying to find Brassyle and that the salt was on board for the ship's 'repair, equipment and maintenance'. He did not dispute that Ireland was not the intended destination or deny that the ships were exploring; he only denied that they were trading. After lengthy court proceedings, including jury deliberations, he was acquitted. But it is far from certain that the truth emerged at Croft's trial.[10] Again, details of this voyage only came to light because Croft came to the attention of the authorities. It is evident that not all voyages from Bristol were recorded, and it is likely that there were others we do not know about.

Jay and Croft must have had a safe harbour in mind when their ships left Bristol. The first Bristol ship to discover Brassyle was indeed looking for trading possibilities as authorized by the licence. Ian Wilson suggests that when the merchants found Brassyle, they would have probably located a safe harbour where they could go ashore and unload their cargo. They may have traded with fishermen who were already there or perhaps they decided to set up their own fishing settlement. They probably built some wooden structures to protect the salt and other supplies from the elements. This would be their base in Brassyle.[11]

As we have seen, when a ship returned to Bristol, the captain reported to the Map Room, where a map was drawn up to show the location and the details of any safe harbours for future use. If Amerike had financed cargo to Brassyle on a regular basis he might have paid for the construction of the shelters on the beach, and the map may have recorded his name written on this harbour: the rutters prepared for skippers who, over many years, hauled Amerike's salt and other goods, may have repeatedly used this name as the unloading point for the cargo.

As other ships were prepared for the voyage to Brassyle, the masters and crews of these vessels would have been briefed in the Map Room and given their rutters and the bills of lading relating to the cargoes they were to deliver. The rutters for a voyage to Brassyle would have been elaborate. The prevailing winds at the latitude of England and Scotland are from the south-west. The rutters would dictate a voyage north towards Iceland, following coastal landmarks around southern Greenland, and across the channel to the Labrador coast. The returning ship could return to Bristol with the prevailing winds and currents across the open ocean, confident of reaching land in about fifteen days.

These Bristol merchants and seamen who delivered cargoes for their employers were neither voyagers nor discoverers.[12] As they fished or traded in the rich new grounds off Newfoundland they were not looking for America, but they might have called their destination the same name as their company, Amerike's safe harbour.

NINE

THE WINTER OF DISCONTENT

For the last seven years the people of Bristol have equipped two, three, or four caravels to go in search of the Island of Brazil and the Seven Cities.

Pedros de Ayala, the Spanish Ambassador to London
reporting to the King and Queen of Spain, 25 July 1498.[1]

The years between 1483 and 1486 were troubled years for England. Since the outbreak of the Wars of the Roses in 1455 a state of civil war existed in which the Houses of Lancaster and York intermittently fought each other for control of the Crown. Over the thirty-year period ending in 1487, five different kings would reign through seven changes of monarch. Three of these kings would die violent deaths.

Many of the citizens of Bristol with political and royal connections were affected by the changes in loyalty, while the merchants had additionally to adjust to the upheavals caused by the loss of the Bordeaux wine trade. In Bristol, as elsewhere, it was wise to keep a low profile. The merchants were politically astute and survived the changes in the royal succession.

One Bristol family, that of Thomas Croft, had strong family ties with Edward of the House of York. The Battle of Mortimer's Cross in 1461, in which Edward defeated King Henry VI, was fought on land owned by the Croft family, close to Croft Castle, near Leominster in Herefordshire. As a result of the battle Henry was deposed, and Edward was crowned King. His wife's sister was married to another Bristolian, Sir Robert Poyntz.[2]

But in 1483 these favourable connections were severed when King Edward died unexpectedly, his young heir was murdered and Richard III ascended the throne. It was not until 1485 that the tide turned again, when Henry, the Earl of Richmond, arrived from France and landed with an army at Milford Haven in South Wales. He marched across Wales to Shropshire and defeated King Richard III at the Battle of Bosworth Field. Richard was killed, and the victorious Richmond was subsequently crowned King Henry VII. This marked the beginning of the Tudor dynasty. The new King claimed descent from ancient British kings and King Arthur through his Welsh grandfather, and he adopted the Welsh dragon as one of the supporters of the royal arms. This was a good time to be a Welsh aristocrat.

There are no port or customs records of any specific voyages to Brassyle between 1481 and 1490, but several events and records indicate that ships may have ventured there throughout these years. Wilson suggests that fishing vessels loaded with salt and supplies in Bristol (and noted in the port records as destined for Ireland) did not return to Bristol for several months. Fishermen were known to have protected their fishing grounds when they find a lucrative area, so they would have had no incentive to divulge where they were going.[3]

If indeed the merchants had discovered Brassyle by 1485 and had imported a limited quantity of fish to Bristol, interest in the fishing possibilities there may have been waning. Supplying fish to Spain may have become less important as the market matured. The merchants may have had trouble justifying the outlay for the small financial return from these voyages.

In 1486, King Henry VII visited Bristol. The new King was anxious to win the support of England's burgeoning merchant class. Foremost on the agenda were the Mare Oceanum voyages, trade, and the role the new government would play. The Bristol merchants used the occasion to complain to the King that the loss of the Icelandic trade was a financial hardship. The King, however, was not sympathetic and observed that their wives seemed to be arrayed in fashionable and expensive finery.

The discovery of Brassyle was not exactly the trading opportunity that the Bristol merchants had hoped for. There is no doubt that the fishing was good. The Bristol merchants had never seen such rich fishing grounds but there was virtually no market for the woollen cloth, the hardware, and the food they hoped to trade with the fishermen selling stockfish. The natives in the new land

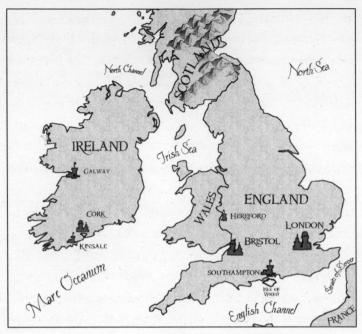

Map of Great Britain and Ireland. (*Courtesy Jeff Reynolds*)

had nothing to trade, and the only supplies they could sell were salt and a few everyday essentials. There was no justification for outfitting a large cargo ship, such as the *Trinity*, to sail to an area that could not absorb any goods and could only offer fish and trees.

The King was keenly aware of the voyages to Brassyle authorized by the trading licence of 1480–3. He was probably aware of the international interest in exploration in the ocean to the west, particularly the discovery and settling of islands, which were so necessary as staging areas and for provisioning ships. The Spanish and Portuguese were discovering islands they would use as stepping-stones to the New World. The King was also acutely concerned about England's relationship with Spain, embodying, as it did, imminent ambitions of expansion. However, the Bristol merchants were showing little interest in establishing a foothold in Brassyle let alone exploring a trade route further west.

The King stayed at the estate of Sir Robert Poyntz at Iron Acton, a few miles north of Bristol. Richard Amerike may have been distantly related to the King through his Welsh aristocratic lineage, and he was also related to the Poyntz family through the marriage in 1343 of Elizabeth Clanvow to Sir John Poyntz.[4]

During the royal visit, Richard Amerike was appointed as the King's Customs Officer, the position Thomas Croft had held earlier. It was a position he would hold several times over the next sixteen years. There are no records of any shipments of dutiable salt cod imported from Brassyle during his period of office, although this is not to say that voyages were not made; as we have seen, if the mariners had caught the fish themselves there would be no duty to pay. But if Bristol merchants were importing fish they had obtained by trading, and it was returned to Bristol, duty should have been levied.

Bartholomew Columbus was by now a merchant dealing internationally in charts and books. In 1488 he sailed to London in an attempt to get sponsorship for his brother. The King rejected Columbus's proposal – perhaps because of commitments he had made to the Bristol merchants.

The King was also in contact with merchant groups in London, where he kept a watchful eye on developments. He made another visit to Bristol in 1490 to discuss these developments and the peace treaty he had reached with the Hanseatic League, according to which the League offered to reopen the Icelandic trade to Bristol merchants. But, interestingly, the merchants were not interested. They were evidently meeting their salted codfish needs from somewhere else and no longer needed to buy fish from Iceland.

Raimondo di Soncino, the Milanese Ambassador to London, would write to his government several years later: 'His companions say that they could bring so many fish that this kingdom would have no further need of Iceland. . .'[5]

Amerike was reappointed to his Customs position during this visit. King Henry again noticed the 'sumptuously apparelled' wives of the merchants. This time he extracted £500 from the Mayor and £1 from each man worth over £200.

Adam's Chronicles of Bristol has this entry for 1490:

This year divers streets in Bristow were new paved, that is to say, Horse Streat, Knight Smith Streat, Brodestreat,

Reclifstreat, St. Thomas Streat, Tuckerstreat, the Backe,
St. Mary Port Streat and Lewins Meade, and the High
Crosse painted and gilded; the doing whereof cost xxl [£20].
And this year the King and the Lord Chancelour came to
Bristow and lay at St. Augustine's. And the commons of
Bristow were made to pay King Henry 5 p Cent. for a
benevalence.[6]

During this visit, the King may have pressured the
Bristol merchants to step up their exploration efforts.
It was after all in the national interest to do so.

From 1490, it appears to have been common
knowledge that several ships ventured across the Mare
Oceanum each year. Pedros de Ayala reported to the
King and Queen of Spain in 1497:

For the last seven years the people of Bristol have
equipped two, three, or four caravels to go in search of
the Island of Brazil and the Seven Cities.[7]

He was reporting on what was probably the departure
of a fishing or trading fleet at the beginning of each
season. Spain, in particular, was paying close attention
to Bristol ship movements and what was happening in
the northern Mare Oceanum.

Thomas Croft died in 1488 at the age of fifty-
three, William Spencer was by now in his seventies,
and the other participants in the Brassyle ventures

were either retiring or had died. (Spencer would die in 1495 and de la Fount a year later.) A new generation of merchants was stepping into the breach. Richard Amerike was in his fifties and, as we have seen, had climbed to a lofty position in local politics. Of the original participants in the 1479–83 expeditions, Amerike was virtually the only prominent member still involved in Bristol's trade and politics.[8]

Indeed, almost all the seafaring community was now drawn from a generation that would have been familiar with the new fishing grounds in Brassyle. A Master Mariner named Hugh Elliot and several members of the prosperous Thorne family were younger merchants now working in the Brassyle trade. Hugh Elliot, accompanied by one of the Thorne family, visited Brassyle during the mid-1490s.[9]

By 1495, the rutters that mariners collected in the Map Room prior to sailing to Brassyle would by now contain fifteen years of accumulated knowledge. There would have been several copies of these books, duplicated by hand. At least four ships were at times making the voyage simultaneously, probably in convoy. However, each captain would have had the full volume on board, and extra copies remained in the Map Room. A mariner of Elliot's stature and competence would have had his own copy, embellished and emended in his own hand.

Because of the increase in the number of voyages, Bristol seamen had ventured westward and had sailed far enough along the coast to determine that Brassyle was perhaps an indeterminate mainland and not an isolated island as was originally believed.[10] Johan Day would write in 1497: '. . . It was called the Island of Brazil, and it is assumed and believed to be the mainland that the men from Bristol found.'[11]

The major headlands, islands and many landmarks would certainly have been named by this time. The large body of land to the west, now referred to as mainland, was 'Brassyle'. But what of the capes, harbours, and settlements they were visiting year after year? Surely the captains and fishermen would have had working names for them by now? Names were not designated out of anecdotal whimsy; they identified important landmarks and destinations. Once chosen, they were written in multiple copies on the rutters so that several pilots travelling in a convoy would have the same information. It is highly probable that, over time, these mapped or locally used names would have become established by usage.

TOSCANELLI'S MAP

. . . to Cristobal Colombo, greeting. I perceive your magnificent and great desire
to find a way to where the spices grow, and in reply to your letter I send you the
copy of another letter which I wrote, some days ago, to a friend and favourite . . .
of the most serene King of Portugal . . . in reply to another which, by direction of
his highness, he wrote to me on [the subject of sailing west from Portugal to
reach the East Indies], and I send you another sea chart like the one I sent him,
by which you will be satisfied respecting your enquiries.

Letter from Toscanelli to Christopher Columbus.[1]

It had long been presumed that the western edge of Europe and Africa formed the western edge of the world.[2] Only when it was realized that the world was a finite globe and the full extent of Asia was known did cosmographers comprehend that if one travelled far enough to the west, across the Mare Oceanum, one would eventually reach Asia from the opposite direction.

By 1450 European travellers had discovered the continents of Europe, Africa, and Asia, including Cathay and Chipanga (which today we call China and Japan), and had produced recognizable maps. These maps, however, were not in general circulation due to the high cost of preparation and limited availability. But while Ptolemy's theory that the earth was at the centre of the universe was still generally unchallenged, and it would be another seventy-five years before Copernicus would understand that the earth revolved around the sun, cosmologists and chart makers were fully aware that the earth was a globe, with cold polar regions and a central parallel of latitude called the equator.

The craft of map-drawing was quite sophisticated at this time. Coastlines were charted on board a ship by triangulating between mountains, headlands and other geographical features. Ships seldom ventured beyond the sight of land, and a ship's master could accurately chart his position by sighting any three features and calculating the angles between them. These techniques enabled map-makers to chart coastlines and, for some, to predict bold new directions.

Paolo dal Pozzo Toscanelli was a brilliant mathematician, astronomer and cosmographer who lived in Florence, where he was a professor at the university. He calculated that the known world of Europe, Africa, and Asia, from Spain to Chipanga, spanned 230 of the 360 degrees of the globe.

Remembering from Marco Polo's accounts that the distance from Spain to Chipanga was approximately 11,000 miles, he calculated that it would only be a distance of 4,000 miles from Spain to the eastern coast of Chipanga if, instead of travelling east, he sailed west across the Mare Oceanum. He further believed that the Island of Antillia, sometimes known as the Island of Seven Cities, was midway between Spain and

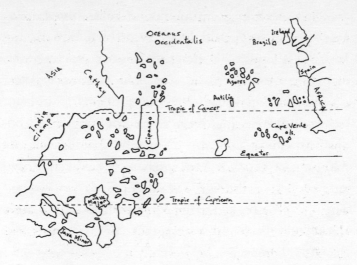

Reconstruction of Toscanelli's map of 1474, based on Martin Behaim's globe. The
map shows Europe and Japan separated by the Mare Oceanum.

Chipanga, thus providing two secure staging points in
the nearly 6,000 miles between Spain and Cathay. He
published a map in 1474 showing an uninterrupted
Mare Oceanum spanning the remaining 130 degrees of
longitude, between Spain and Chipanga.

Lisbon cathedral's Canon, Fernao Martinez, had met
Paolo Toscanelli during an earlier visit to Italy and was
familiar with his teachings. At the request of King
Alfonzo V of Portugal, Canon Martinez wrote to
Toscanelli and requested details of his theory of sailing
west to Cathay. Toscanelli replied in a letter dated
25 June 1474, with which he included a map. Toscanelli
was eager to have the Portuguese authorities prove his

theory, which he communicated to Canon Fernao Martinez, who could use his influence with the Portuguese Crown.[3] Columbus also gained access to this map; he corresponded with Toscanelli several years later.

The error in Toscanelli's mathematics would not become apparent for thirty years. The longitude from Spain to Chipanga is approximately 150 degrees, not 230, so completing an encirclement of the earth would entail travelling through 210 degrees, rather than 130. The distance from Spain to Chipanga, sailing west through the Panama Canal, is therefore nearer 12,000 than 4,000 miles.

The circumference of the earth at the equator is therefore much greater than Toscanelli thought. He estimated it to be 18,000 miles when in fact it is 24,902 miles. It is widely believed that Toscanelli may have been a teacher of Amerigo Vespucci when Vespucci was a student in Florence. Ironically, it was Amerigo Vespucci who would discover the true distance. In 1502 he took accurate observations and calculated the circumference of the earth at the equator to within an accuracy of 50 miles.[4]

In 1490, two years before Columbus sailed west, Martin Behaim produced a globe based on Toscanelli's map. It showed Europe, Africa, and Asia, with the Mare Oceanum separating Europe and Chipanga. The world was a small one for the unfolding sphere of exploration and the colourful cast of characters involved, and this was the world that Christopher Columbus set out to explore in 1492 when he crossed the Mare Oceanum from Spain to the Caribbean Islands.

Columbus continued to believe until the day he died that the world was as shown on Toscanelli's map and Martin Behaim's globe. When he made landfall he had every reason to believe that he had reached one of the many islands shown, to the south-east of Cathay and east of the Malaysian peninsula. His frustration at not being able to find the strait at the Cape of Catigara and the westward passage through the landmass to India can only be imagined.

ELEVEN

A SECRET MAP

Donation 'to the ffryres at our lady of Rebedewe to pray ffor us'.

From the Accounts of the Trinity of Bristol:
donation to the Friary of
Santa Maria de la Rabida, Huelva, Spain, 1480.[1]

Shortly after Columbus returned to Lisbon in 1477 his brother joined him there, and they both initially worked as chart makers. They also started a small commercial business and very likely had contact with Bristol ships and the local agents of Bristol merchants. During his first two years in Lisbon, Columbus travelled frequently to Genoa and Madeira, trading in sugar.

He soon met Felipa Moniz Perestrella, the aristocratic daughter of an Italian diplomat who was living in Lisbon with his Portuguese wife. Columbus and Felipa married in 1479, and a year later they had a son, Diego. This marriage gave Columbus Portuguese citizenship, which afforded him the right to trade in Africa.[2]

With the sea in his blood, his attentions turned to the south. Both the Spanish and Portuguese governments were backing exploration along the African coast in the hope that they could open up a trade route around the African continent to India and Cathay.

Portugal was in conflict with the Castilian government over the control of the Cape Verde Islands, which are situated some 300 miles off the west coast of Africa. Castilian forces occupied the islands between 1477 and 1479 and began attacking Portuguese ships sailing between Lisbon and the Guinea coast of West Africa. To avoid this threat, Portuguese ships began to give the Cape Verde Islands a wide berth to the west.

This manoeuvre necessitated being at sea and out of the sight of land for about five days. Such an endeavour required advanced navigation skills based on reading the stars and working with compass bearings. Columbus is believed to have been on at least one of these trips to the Guinea coast of Africa and several to Madeira during this time.

In the sea off the Cape Verde Islands hurricanes form several times each autumn and travel in a westerly direction to the Caribbean. The tropical ocean currents also follow a similar path. A Portuguese ship returning from West Africa to Lisbon, fortunately laden with food and provisions, is believed to have strayed into one such hurricane and to have found itself several days later at Hispaniola in the Caribbean Islands. The ship eventually made its way back to Lisbon, and a rough map of its circuitous route is reputed to have been produced by someone in the crew.[3]

The ship first went south to the Venezuelan coast and worked its way west and north into the Caribbean

1 Waldseemüller World Map of 1507. (*The British Library*)

2 Vespucci: detail from the Waldseemüller World Map of 1507. (*The British Library*)

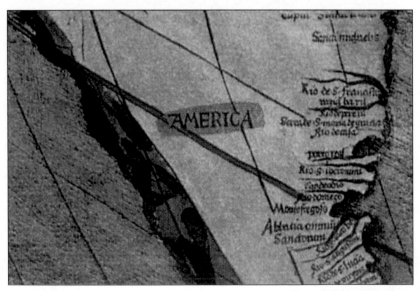

3 America: detail from the Waldseemüller World Map of 1507. (*The British Library*)

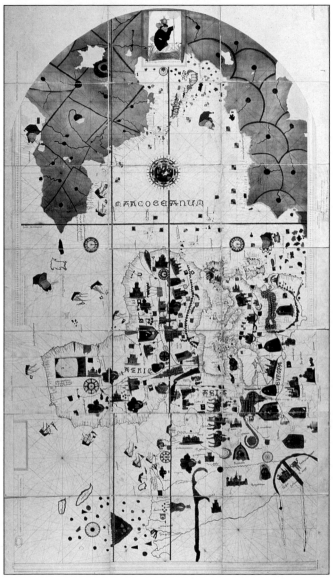

4 Juan de la Cosa's Map of the Old and New Worlds, *c.* 1500. Five English flags are drawn along the eastern seaboard of North America, with the notation, 'sea discovered by the English'. (*Museo Naval, Madrid*)

5 *The Departure of John
and Sebastian Cabot from
Bristol on their first Voyage
of Discovery, 1497, c.
1906, oil on canvas by
Ernest Board 1877-1934.
(Bridgeman Art
Library / Bristol City
Museum and Art Gallery)*

6 *Departure from Lisbon for Brazil, the East Indies and America:* engraving by Theodore de Bry, illustrated in Chapter 1 of *Americae Tertia Pars,* 1562. *(Service Historique de la Marine, Vincennes / Bridgeman Art Library / Lauros / Giraudon)*

7 St Mary Redcliffe, watercolour on paper, John Sell Cotman c. 1802. (*Bridgeman Art Library / Private collection*)

9 Amerike coat of arms, the Lord Mayor's Chapel, Bristol.

10 The *Matthew*: reconstruction. (*Courtesy of The Matthew of Bristol*)

Sea before heading into the Mare Oceanum, seeing the tip of Cuba on the way. Most of the crew died from disease, and the ship was severely damaged from the ravages of storms and teredos.

While Columbus was working in Lisbon in 1479 he is believed to have met a Portuguese sailor who had survived this voyage and obtained or prepared a copy of the map. The map was not complete but showed coastline and islands seen by the sailors, suggesting that there were many islands about 750 lcagues, or 2,500 miles, west of Spain.

Two years later, Toscanelli sent Columbus a copy of his map, explaining the details he had already given to the Canon of Lisbon that Chipanga was 4,000 miles west of Spain, and Cathay was a further 1,500 miles beyond that.[4]

Columbus thought that Toscanelli had overestimated the distance. He was convinced he would reach the mysterious Island of Seven Cities after about 2,500 miles and that Chipanga would be just another 1,000 miles. This, he believed, was confirmed by the 'secret' map he had obtained, and he deduced that he could sail west for 2,500 miles and reach islands that were in the vicinity of the Island of Seven Cities.

At the age of thirty-one, Columbus had sailed east to Turkey and perhaps as far north as the Arctic Circle. He had sailed as far south along the African coast as

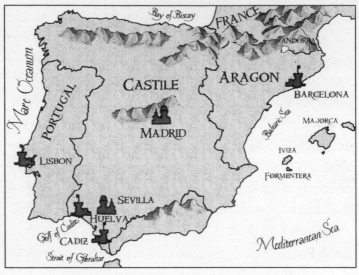

Map of Spain and Portugal. (*Courtesy of Jeff Reynolds*)

any European had gone at that time. He had learned about the prevailing winds, how they blew onshore from the west, north of the Straits of Gibraltar; and how this reversed to be offshore at the latitudes of Africa. From his personal exploits, he knew there was a fortune to be made by opening up trade routes to Cathay, Chipanga, and India by sailing westwards. An ambitious plan was formulating in his head.

In 1484 he approached King Joao II of Portugal for sponsorship. However, Columbus's demands were quite brash, bordering on the insolent. He insisted on one-third of all profits from the resulting trade and extraordinary recognition for his contribution.

The royal court in Portugal did not have much faith in Columbus's scheme. The prevailing winds are onshore in Portugal, and the concept of battling headwinds for 4,000 miles did not seem realistic to the authorities.

Columbus was still working as a map-maker in Lisbon in 1484 when his wife died. The political climate, ever sensitive to intrigue, had deteriorated to an alarming degree. The King executed two friends and political acquaintances of his wife's family, the Duke of Braganza in 1483 and the Duke of Viseu (the Queen's brother) in 1484. Late in 1485 Columbus decided to leave Portugal and, availing himself of an opportune connection, he moved to Spain.[5]

His deceased wife's family lived nearby and he stayed at the Franciscan monastery of Santa Maria de la Rabida at Huelva. He became close friends with the Abbot, Juan Perez, and agreed to settle his five-year-old son, Diego, there for the time being. Thus began Columbus's long relationship with the monastery, where he would intermittently live and study for extended periods.

Huelva, Seville's ocean port, was a centre of learning. The monastery welcomed sailors from visiting ships, and many gladly accepted the accommodation that was provided there while their ships were laid up in port.[6]

After a few months, Columbus moved to Cadiz, where he was employed by the Duke of Medinaceli. This gave him access to the court, and in 1487 he began seven years of employment with Spain's royal bureaucracy. He

La Rabida Friary. (*Rodney Broome*)

received a small salary, the equivalent of a seaman's wage, and worked as a merchant disposing of war booty after the Spanish had captured Malaga from Moorish control and enslaved its Muslim population.

Columbus returned frequently to la Rabida to visit his son. He spent many hours discussing cosmography with Father Marchina, and it was here that his plans to sail to India across the Mare Oceanum were nurtured. The Abbot, Juan Perez, became one of Columbus's strongest advocates.[7]

Merchant ships from Bristol, including the *Trinity*, called at the Friary every few months and Columbus would have been particularly interested in what he could learn about the success the Bristol ships were experiencing in their efforts to locate Brassyle and other islands. Father Marchina, who was a friend and confessor to many of the sailors, was undoubtedly a wealth of information.

TWELVE

THE OCEAN BLUE

*And there had beene before that time (1492) a discoverie of some Lands, which they
tooke to bee islands, and were indeed the Continent of America, towards the Northwest.
And it may be that some Relation of this nature comming afterwards to the knowledge
of Columbus, and by him suppressed (desirous rather to make his Enterprise the Child
of his Science and Fortune, then the Follower of a former Discoverie), did give him
better assurance, that all was not Sea, from the west of Europe and Africke unto Asia.*

The History of the Reign of
King Henrie the Seventh. Francis Bacon, 1622.[1]

After the English Crown rejected Columbus's plea
for sponsorship in 1488, he again sought the
patronage of the Queen of Spain, but without success.
In 1491 he discussed this with the Abbot of Huelva,
where his son still lived. Soon after, the Abbot met the
Queen and advocated Columbus's case. He related that
Columbus was ready to leave Spain and go to England
where he felt sure he could convince King Henry VII to
support him. The Queen told the Abbot that when
Spain had finally expelled the Moors from Castile and
had driven them back to North Africa, she would
consider his plea with commitment.

Granada, the Moorish capital, fell in February 1491.
True to her word, Queen Isabella arranged to finance
Columbus, even agreeing to his exorbitant terms.

Columbus's Ship. (Reproduced in Roselly de Lorgnes, *Vie et Voyages de Christophe Colomb*, Paris.).

Columbus had his ships provisioned by the Medici Bank in Seville, where a young banker named Amerigo Vespucci made the appropriate arrangements.

On 3 August 1492, Columbus left the Spanish port of Palos with three ships: the *Nina*, the *Pinta*, and the *Santa Maria*. They sailed south-west to the Canary Islands from where they turned and headed due west across the Mare Oceanum. Columbus knew that the trade winds in the latitudes of the Canaries would be astern, blowing him south and west into the unknown world beyond the atlas.

During the voyage, Columbus privately referred to his secret map, from which he had calculated the length of the sea crossing and the time it would take. The *Santa Maria* was navigated by its owner, Juan de la Cosa, who would later publish a map that is still controversial (see Plate 4).

On 12 October they sighted land and arrived on the island of San Salvador in the Caribbean. Columbus was convinced that they had reached some islands that were near to Chipanga, or Zipangu, and to the east of Indo-China, an area thought to have been within the sphere of India. He immediately referred to the location as the 'Indies', and he called the inhabitants 'Indians'.

He then sailed on to Cuba, which he believed was Zipangu: '. . . all my globes and world maps seem to

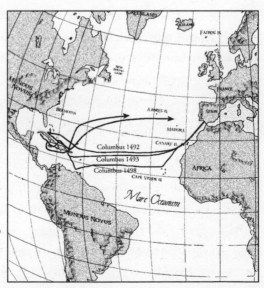

Map of Columbus's first three voyages to the New World. (*Courtesy of Jeff Reynolds*)

indicate that the island of Japan is in this vicinity and I am sure that Cuba and Zipangu are one'. They looked in vain for gold. They determined that the mainland of Cathay would lie to the west.[2]

Referring to Toscanelli's map, Columbus believed he would be able to sail west along the south coast of Cathay for about 1,500 miles, which might take three or four weeks, and then follow the coastline south for a similar distance along the east coast of Indo-China, or Vietnam, as it is known today. At the southern end of this peninsula was the Strait of Catigara, between Indo-China and Sumatra. Marco Polo had sailed through this strait 200 years earlier and had camped on the beach on Sumatra for five months, waiting for the monsoons to end so his fleet could continue on a north-west heading to India. Columbus knew from Polo's writings that it was a nineteen-day sail to the River Ganges in India from Sumatra.

On 24 December the *Santa Maria* ran aground on a reef on Hispaniola and was broken up by the surf. The crew was left on the island to be picked up the following year. Columbus sailed east across the ocean with the prevailing westerly winds behind him and arrived back in Spain on 15 March 1493, stepping ashore in Palos, near Huelva. The King and Queen were at the other end of the country in Barcelona, and Columbus, enlivened by his success, seized the opportunity to parade his exotic cavalcade. He immediately set out overland to report to the Catholic Monarchs. This trip took him through many towns, including the port of Valencia, where his entourage, complete with parrots, wondrous plants and Indians, paraded through the streets. (A certain John Caboto witnessed this outlandish cavalcade.) When he arrived in Barcelona, Columbus reported to the authorities that he had reached islands off the coast of Cathay and Indo-China.

Spain laid claim to these new discoveries, a stance supported by the Pope. In their aggressive competition for territory to the south and the west of Europe, Spain and Portugal finally agreed in 1493 to divide the globe equally along a line of longitude some 300 miles west of the Cape Verde Islands, and, according to the terms of this agreement, Spain could claim all non-Christian lands west of that line. At the Treaty of Tordesillas in 1494 the line of longitude was moved westwards to 370 leagues to the west of the Cape Verde Islands. This had the effect of giving most of the New World to Spain, while Brazil, Africa and India fell to Portugal.

Motivated by the prospect of wealth, Columbus immediately planned another voyage. This expedition was larger and better equipped. On 25 September 1493 he sailed again, this time with 17 ships, 1,500 men, and livestock. He established a community on Hispaniola and visited Santo Domingo and Puerto

Rico, returning to Spain nearly three years later on 11 June 1496 with 500 slaves, gold and tobacco.[3]

On his first voyage to the Caribbean in 1492, Columbus appeared to know exactly where he was going, and it seemed to his crew and associates that he was continually attempting to fit his discoveries into some preconceived map. On subsequent visits, he consistently refused to accept that Cuba was an island, and forbade anyone to sail west along the southern shore to prove the contrary.

THIRTEEN

CABOT'S VOYAGES

Henry, by the grace of God, king of England and France, and lord of Ireland, . . .
Be it knowen that we have given and granted . . . to our well beloved John Cabot
citizen of Venice, full and free authority to saile to all parts, countreys, and seas
of the East, of the West, and of the North, under our banners and ensigns, . . . and
have given licence to set up our . . . banners and ensigns in any town, city, castle,
island or mainland whatsoever, newly found by them. . . .

Letters patent granted to John Cabot
by King Henry VII, 5 March 1496.[1]

In 1493 John Cabot, an experienced Italian mariner, was living in Valencia. In April of that year, Columbus passed through Valencia after his first voyage to the Caribbean on his way from Seville to Barcelona. Cabot spent part of his early childhood in Genoa, where the Cabot and Columbus families may have known each other. But John grew up mainly on the streets and canals of Venice, where his family moved in 1461. His father was a merchant.

Like Columbus, Cabot had ambitions to sail to the Orient across the Mare Oceanum. He was already well travelled and had been as far east as Mecca. He correctly believed that it would be a much shorter distance to Asia at a more northerly latitude, and he tried to persuade Spanish and Portuguese merchants to sponsor him in exploring a more northerly route than Columbus had taken. He was unsuccessful.

Cabot realized that neither Spain nor Portugal would be likely to sponsor him once Queen Isabella had offered Columbus her patronage. He therefore decided to approach the English government, reasoning that this would afford an opportunity for England to catch up with Spain and Portugal without getting into a competitive situation or even a naval confrontation over potential land claims in the southerly latitudes.

Very soon after Columbus had passed through Valencia, Cabot sailed with his family to Bristol. Cabot was using the same Behaim globe that Columbus had relied on, and he expected to sail about 1,500 miles from England and arrive at the coast of Cathay by using this northerly latitude. It is probable that Cabot had also heard that Bristol merchant ships were regularly crossing the open seas to the Island of Brassyle, which he calculated to be near the north-east coast of Cathay.

Cabot thought that the Bristol merchants might be persuaded to take him to Brassyle on an officially sanctioned expedition. At worst, he believed their fishing base could provide a safe harbour and staging area for further exploration. His contacts in Bristol guaranteed financial support and were sufficiently influential to obtain letters patent.

No doubt the King and the English government realized the potential for controlling a northern trade route to Cathay. By cunning and diplomacy, they might be able to claim new territory without competing with Spain. The King was particularly anxious not to antagonize Spain. He was negotiating a marriage between his son Arthur and Catherine of Aragon. The marriage took place in 1501, but Arthur died the following year. When Henry VIII inherited the throne in 1509, he married his deceased brother's widow, who thus became the first of his six wives.

The Bristol merchants appeared focused only on the immediate trade opportunities. They had failed to find any cities or large communities with which to trade during their explorations along the coast.

The Crown was not unduly concerned about having a foreigner in control of this voyage, whose purpose was to stake a land claim. The Bristol merchants with their trading licence had long since decided that there was no pressing reason to claim Brassyle for England.

Cabot's goal was primarily to open a trade route to Cathay. In his view, any claims to land were secondary considerations, important only in so far as they would strengthen control of the lucrative trade routes. Cabot, like Columbus, was driven by the promise of personal wealth: his aim was to open up trade routes to the spice and silk markets in the Orient.

Cabot obtained the necessary letters patent, which were issued at an audience with King Henry VII on 5 March 1496. It was stipulated that he could take five ships, that he must stay to the north and that he must go from and return to Bristol.

Several influential merchants and politicians had the connections in London and probably made the application for this document, just as they had obtained the trading licence in 1480. Richard Amerike was himself a wealthy merchant and had been Customs Officer for ten years. He was in the perfect position to make the arrangements.

An expedition like this was expensive, and the Bristol merchants only put one ship at Cabot's disposal. It was probably a 3-masted, 50-tun caravel measuring about 70 feet in length. Setting off most likely in the summer of 1496, Cabot was undoubtedly disappointed that the Bristol merchants would not provide the security of at least a second ship. Perhaps other ships of the Bristol fishing fleet had already left for Brassyle and the master of Cabot's ship was confident that he could meet up with them if the situation required. Cabot's ship left Bristol and headed over the well-travelled route towards Ireland, past the Faeroes, and on towards Iceland. The prevailing winds at these latitudes were from the south-west. Sailing north kept land in sight and avoided bucking head winds.

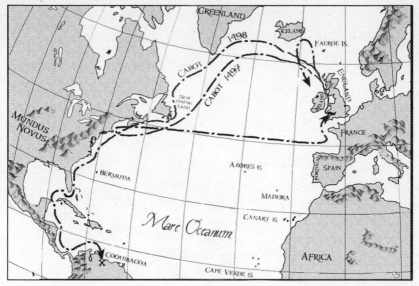

Possible Routes of Cabot's Voyages in 1496, 1497 and 1498. (*Courtesy of Jeff Reynolds*)

Cabot was accompanied by his barber, the only person on board with whom he could communicate. He spoke Genoese Italian and Spanish, and the Bristol men spoke in a strong regional English dialect. Even an Englishman from London would have had a difficult time understanding them.

Relations on board the ship were strained. The weather was severe, with crashing storms and ice-cold rain beating down on the crew. The men were concerned about ice building up in the rigging and the possibility of the ship capsizing. Unused to sailing in icy conditions, Cabot may not have appreciated the

'A storm hits the caravels', engraving by M. Rouargue, reproduced in Roselly de Lorgnes, *Vie et Voyages de Christophe Colomb*, Paris.

danger. He was a skilled mariner who was well schooled in all kinds of navigation and probably wanted to navigate by the stars. The merchants may have intentionally confused Cabot for misguided or xenophobic reasons. They probably did not want a foreigner learning too much about their business.

For whatever reasons, communication and teamwork were at a low ebb, and the ship did not even get as far as Iceland. When the weather turned violent, Cabot gave the order to turn back to Bristol. The only record of this voyage is contained in this extract from a letter by Johan Day, written after a second voyage, in which he relates:

> Since your Lordship wants information relating to the first voyage, here is what happened: he went with one ship, his crew confused him, he was short of supplies and he ran into bad weather, and he decided to turn back.[2]

A few months later, in the spring of 1497, a second attempt was made in a ship called the *Matthew*. Again, they sailed with only one ship. A Bristol pilot and two Bristol merchants were in charge of the ship. That such experienced and wealthy merchants would embark on a potentially dangerous transoceanic voyage with one small 70-foot vessel shows the high level of confidence they had in their ships, their sailing abilities, and their knowledge of where they were going. But they had been authorized to take five ships, and a prudent mariner would have taken at least two or three as a contingency, in case disaster struck. The decision to sail in one ship, and a relatively small one at that, may also indicate that the merchants were unwilling to invest much in a venture when they were so sceptical about the profitability of such an exploratory trip to a land they knew was not the promised spice kingdom. Again, perhaps they also knew that other Bristol ships would be in the area if the need arose to get help. During this exploratory mission, the merchants very likely purposely avoided their own fishing grounds. Under these circumstances, there would be no justification for sending more than one ship or even a larger vessel.

A typical cargo would have consisted of barrels of beer and wine and a quantity of salt. Water, stored on board in barrels, would usually be undrinkable after a week. Barrels of dried beans, dried peas, salted meats, fish, vegetables, small pigs, some chickens, and enough food for seven or eight months were loaded into the hold.

On 2 May 1497 the *Matthew* sailed from Bristol's Redcliffe Wharf. Fourteen Bristol crewmen sailed the ship. Cabot was accompanied by his barber and a merchant from Burgundy.[3] Other ships of the Bristol fishing fleet had probably already left for Brassyle, and his conspiring crew, made up of local seamen, knew that it was important that Cabot did not see them or know where they were going. The *Matthew* went via Bantry Bay on the west coast of Ireland on the route to the fishing grounds of Iceland, then due west, skirting the southern coast of Greenland.

Again, there were conflicts between the Bristol crew and Cabot. The *Matthew* sailed south of the fishing grounds off the coast of Newfoundland. This may have been by design if they did not want Cabot to observe the fishing area.

On the other hand, Cabot, with his navigation skills and knowledge of Toscanelli's map, may have been confident that they could stay to the south in the open sea and approach the mainland of Brassyle further to the west.

The crossing from Ireland was relatively easy with only one gale. After thirty-four days, they sighted land, most likely in the vicinity of Maine, or Cape Breton. The coast was heavily forested with tall straight trees, and the weather was clear. This suggests that they were considerably west of Newfoundland, which is more lightly forested and usually foggy in the summer. They noted that the trees would be a good source of timber from which to make ship masts. Again Johan Day mentioned this in his letter, stating that:

> . . . they found tall trees of the kind masts are made, and other smaller trees, and the country is very rich in grass.[4]

The Bristol merchants knew exactly where they were. They saw evidence of fish drying on racks on the beaches and other evidence of human habitation. Cabot cautiously went ashore on 24 June, staying within bowshot range of the ship in case there were hostile natives. He planted the royal ensign and claimed the land for England.

The ship's master had been issued his rutters in Bristol, and he may also have had his own rudimentary charts. Cabot no doubt was anxious to see and copy them. The Bristol men would also have their own names for many places, and these names may have been in the records on board the ship.

The crew fished and salted cod to take back to Bristol. Cabot wrote about the fish to his friend Raimondo di Soncino, who in turn quoted Cabot in another letter to the Duke of Milan in December 1497 (see page 65).

The *Matthew* then sailed east along the coast for a month, most likely past Nova Scotia, New Brunswick, and the southern coast of Newfoundland. Cabot drew extensive charts of about 900 miles of coastline. He was convinced that he had reached an island or an extension of land off the Cathay mainland.

On his own map, Cabot named the initial landing area 'Prima Vista', and he identified the mainland as 'Brassyle'. A nearby island was named 'St John's Island' because 24 June is St John's Day. He thought the large island to the east (which may have been New Brunswick) must be the Island of Seven Cities. He named several capes and landmarks, some of them after friends and acquaintances. The name 'Cape St George' survives to this day and may have originated from this voyage.

After leaving the coast, they sailed back to England, arriving in Bristol only fifteen days later on 6 August 1497.

Just as they had done on the outward voyage, the crew misled Cabot on the homeward crossing by swinging further to the south than their usual route. Confident that they would reach land in France, they did not worry that they were well off course. When they sighted the coast of Brittany, they established their location and sailed north to England.

After returning to Bristol, Cabot and the merchants immediately went to London. Just three days after docking in Bristol, they were granted an audience with King Henry VII. The Spanish envoy, Pedros de Ayala, attended the meeting, to which Cabot brought his map and a globe showing the part of Cathay they had visited and how near they were to the spice and silk markets. The King renamed the new territory 'New founde land' at this meeting, and he awarded Cabot a pension of £10 for that year. This was subsequently raised to £20 a year on 13 December of the same year.

Cabot's contribution to the Brassyle venture had been to identify Brassyle in the global picture. It was surely a part of north-east Cathay, and it would just be a short journey down the coast to the large cities of Cathay. The silk and spice markets were almost within reach.

After his audience with the King, the party returned to Bristol where Cabot was fêted as a hero, dressed in silk and called 'the Great Admiral'. Cabot celebrated his discovery by bestowing titles and land to friends and naming landmarks in the newly recognized land. Raimondo di Soncino wrote to the Duke of Milan:

> I have also spoken with a Burgundian, who was a companion of Messer Zoanne (Cabot) . . . the Admiral (for so Messer Zoanne is entitled) has given him an island, and has given another to his barber of Castione, who is a Genoese, and both look upon themselves as Counts . . . some poor Italian friars . . . have all had the promise of being bishops.[5]

Alfred Hudd speculated that the name America, or a similar word derived from the surname of Richard Amerike, was written on this map by John Cabot. Hudd thought that Cabot might have honoured Amerike for his role as Customs Officer, but he was probably unaware of the earlier voyages from Bristol to Brassyle and Amerike's career as a successful merchant.

Cabot's map does not exist today, so nobody knows for certain which names he included on it. But Day wrote:

> . . . for in it [the map] are named the capes of the mainland and the islands, and thus you will see where land was first sighted. . . .

At the time, everyone was convinced that Cabot and his party had visited the east coast of Cathay. No one gave thought to the concept that a new continent had been discovered and it would be six years before this belief would be challenged.

King Henry was so enthusiastic about Cabot's discovery that a third, far better equipped voyage was immediately planned for the next year. More letters patent were issued on 3 February 1498, authorizing Cabot to take six ships, each of up to 200 tuns, and to explore the coastline south from Newfoundland to where the Spanish were concentrating their activities. Raimondo di Soncino sums up Cabot's ambition in the same letter quoted earlier:

> By this means they hope to make London a more important mart for spices than Alexandria.[6]

Cabot's map from his 1497 voyage was seen and copied by several people. To make their claim to the land, the English government had to allow representatives of foreign powers to see it. Pedros de Ayala wrote a detailed report to his government in July 1498 in which he said that he had seen Cabot's maps and that he was aware of Bristol ships sailing to Brassyle for seven years prior to Cabot's voyage (see Appendix A).

Columbus and Vespucci did not have to wait for the Spanish government to report to them on what Ayala had seen on Cabot's map. In 1955 the almost incredible discovery was made that a merchant in Bristol sent Columbus a copy of Cabot's map (see Appendix B). Johan Day wrote to Christopher Columbus:

> I am sending you a copy [map] of the land which has been found.

Columbus had possession of Cabot's map before he sailed on his third voyage to the Caribbean in 1498, while Amerigo Vespucci had until the spring of 1499 to study it.[7]

RACE TO THE ORIENT

It is certain that Hojeda in his first voyage encountered certain Englishmen in the vicinity of Coquibacoa.

Martin Fernandez de Navarette,
Spanish historian, 1829.[1]

In May 1498, both Columbus and Cabot coincidentally sailed west to the New World, both intent on completing their sea routes to India and Cathay. Columbus sailed from Spain with six ships, while Cabot sailed from Bristol with five. Cabot left with the declared intention of sailing to the island and mainland he visited the previous year and then travelling from there, west and then south, along the coast of the land of the Great Khan. He stated his intention to continue to the Tropics.[2]

Cabot's fleet consisted of one large ship provided by the King at a cost of £113 8s and furnished by Lancelot Thirkill, a London merchant. Bristol traders provided four smaller merchant ships.[3] The ships were loaded with 'slight and gross merchandises, as coarse cloth caps, laces, points, and other trifles, to trade with Indians'.[4] In total there were 300 men on board the ships. The cargo indicated that the expedition expected to meet and trade with Indians, an assumption that Cabot himself would not have made as a result of his own experience the previous year.

A few days after leaving Bristol, one of the ships was damaged by a storm off the Irish coast, and eventually returned to England. The citizens of Bristol would have expected Cabot's fleet to return within two or three years; but nothing was ever heard from them again. The entire fleet disappeared without trace. However, there were a few clues.

In *The Columbus Myth* Ian Wilson explores what he thinks may have happened during Cabot's last voyage. The remaining four ships sailed the usual northern route, skirting Greenland and reaching the coast of the New World in the vicinity of Labrador and the north-east coast of Newfoundland. Cabot had not been this far north in 1497. The ship then sailed south along the Atlantic coast of Newfoundland. At Grates Cove, near the south-eastern tip of Newfoundland, one of the ships may have struck a rock and broken up, the crew perhaps making it to shore.

Five years later, Gaspar Corte Real, a Portuguese navigator, rounded up fifty native Beothuks at Grates Cove and took them prisoner to be sold as slaves. One had in his possession a broken Venetian sword and another an Italian earring.[5]

Cabot was not at the mercy of a few Bristol merchants on this expedition. If there were fishing boats, he may have seen them. Perhaps they visited a familiar safe harbour where salt had been delivered and stored, and Cabot may have included it and its name on his charts.

The fleet, or the three ships that now remained, rounded Newfoundland and sailed west passing the coast they had surveyed the previous year. They continued west and south charting the present day United States eastern seaboard, all the time looking for signs of Cathay. They landed and went ashore in several places. Many weeks later they reached the southernmost point of the mainland, and the evidence suggests that they sailed west towards the Gulf of Mexico, and eventually the Caribbean Sea.

In just twelve months, the concept of Brassyle being a remote island had changed. It was evidently adjacent to a very large landmass. Perhaps the Bristol merchants had been right after all when they had abandoned notions of finding cities with which to trade. By August 1499, if Wilson's theory is correct, Cabot's fleet was sailing east along the north coast of what is now Venezuela.

Just four months earlier, in May, four caravels set sail from Cadiz under the command of the 29-year-old Spanish Admiral Alonzo Hojeda. Second in command was Juan de la Cosa, who had sailed and owned the *Santa Maria* in Columbus's first expedition in 1492. He was now nearly fifty years old. Also on board was Amerigo Vespucci.[6]

Hojeda was by all accounts a ruthless and cruel leader, and his behaviour during this voyage would prove no exception. One of his ships was not to his liking, so Hojeda put into port and appropriated another ship by force, leaving the first ship in exchange. He tricked several ships into letting himself and a band of his men board from a rowing boat, and once on board, they robbed the ships. In the Canary Islands they looted the house of Dona Ines de Peranza, the daughter of Columbus's mistress, Dona Beatriz Enriquez de Arana.

Hojeda's fleet crossed the Mare Oceanum and arrived on the New World coast near the mouth of the River Orinoco and then sailed westwards along the coast, robbing, fighting and killing many of the natives they encountered. One settlement they burned to the ground. In the Gulf of Maracaibo they fell upon a coastal village built on stilts in the swampland. They robbed the villagers of their gold in a house-to-house search, killed a score of the native men and kidnapped a young girl.

When they reached Coquibacoa in August, they are believed to have met what was left of Cabot's fleet, which was sailing east towards them.

Malaria, disease, and teredos had taken their toll. What happened to Cabot's men was not documented,

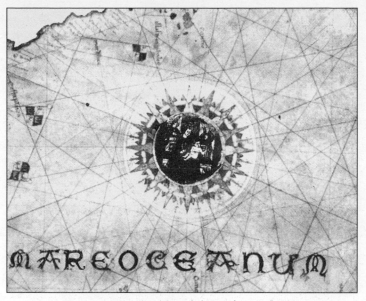

Mare Oceanum: detail from de la Cosa's map of 1500.
(Museo Naval, Madrid)

but evidence indicates that they were slaughtered by Hojeda's forces.

Admiral Hojeda, far from being condemned for his atrocities, was actually rewarded by the Spanish Crown for his patriotic work in stopping the English encroachment from the north. He was awarded grants of land, the title 'Governor of Coquibacoa' and was given instructions to proceed with his discoveries:

that you go and follow the coast which you have discovered, which runs east and west, as it appears, because it goes towards the region where it has been learned that the English were making discoveries . . . in order that it be known that you have discovered that land, so that you may stop the exploration of the English in that direction.[7]

Further reference to Hojeda's battle with Cabot is contained in a licence awarded to him at a later date:

Likewise their Majesties make you a gift in the island of Hispaniola of six leagues of land . . . for the stopping of the English, and the six leagues of land shall be yours forever.[8]

The news of any such battle, however, would never reach Bristol, and Cabot's fate has remained a mystery.

A Spanish historian, Martin Fernandez de Navarette, wrote in 1829: 'It is certain that Hojeda in his first voyage encountered certain Englishmen in the vicinity of Coquibacoa.'[9] Other than the Cabot expedition, there were no other English expeditions in that area at that time. Navarette's source is unknown, but he was a widely respected historian in his day.

If this scenario does depict what happened, Amerigo Vespucci and Juan de la Cosa may have been present at this ghastly deed. Cabot's maps may have been taken in the encounter and this would be the second time that Cabot's extraordinary efforts to produce a map of the New World would end up in the hands of the Spanish.

Admiral Hojeda's encounter was the last time anyone saw Cabot's crew alive. Cabot was trespassing on land that had been deemed Spanish by a papal edict. Hojeda wanted to prevent England from making any claims that would conflict with Spanish ambitions.

From Venezuela, Hojeda and de la Cosa sailed north with two of the ships and joined Columbus at the settlement he had established at Hispaniola. The ships had to be laid up to repair damage they had suffered, some say resulting from the battle with Cabot.

Vespucci, an Italian gentleman, may have had enough of the violence he had been obliged to witness. He left Hojeda and sailed with a second ship south-east along the north coast of what is now Brazil. He believed that the coastline he was following was that of the Gardens of Catigara, or what we call today, Vietnam, and which is identified on Ptolemy's map. He thought that he would eventually reach the southernmost point of the peninsula at what he named the Cape of Catigara and from there be able to sail north-west to India in about nineteen days.

Vespucci happened to have with him some astronomical charts for the Italian city of Ferrara. He was becalmed for almost a month at a point along the Brazilian coast and he used this time to calculate his position in longitude by comparing the movements of the planet Mars with where it would be if he were in Ferrara. According to the charts, on 23 August 1499, Mars was projected to be in conjunction with the moon at approximately fifteen minutes before midnight. Where Vespucci was positioned, this had occurred several hours earlier: in fact, it had occurred before the moon had risen, which was ninety minutes after sunset. Using his observations, he was able to accurately measure the time difference and mathematically calculate his distance from Italy. This was how he discovered the key to calculating the exact size of our terrestrial globe.[10]

Juan de la Cosa returned to Spain with Hojeda, arriving in the port of Santa Maria in July 1500. De la Cosa drew his map of the Caribbean and the New World while his ship was moored in the harbour there. It shows details of English landings along the eastern seaboard of the landmass to the north.

The coastline west of Coquibacoa is drawn with surprising accuracy, in spite of the fact that de la Cosa had not ventured that far west. Indeed, the first map shows a definitive coastline around Florida and the north shore of the Gulf of Mexico. Officially, no European visited that area until 1513. This map is the earliest surviving one of the area. Written in the corner is: 'This map was made by Juan de la Cosa, at Puerto de Santa Maria, in 1500'.[11]

Juan de la Cosa's map (see Plate 4), which is now displayed in the Naval Museum in Madrid, shows the east coast of the New World with English flags in five locations along with the words '*mar descubierto par inglese*' ('sea discovered by the English'). The English flags may well have represented Cabot's landings. This map also shows Cuba as an island. Columbus had insisted it was connected to the mainland.

Vespucci, meanwhile, continued south-eastwards along the Brazilian coast, and he is credited with discovering the mouth of the River Amazon. His ships eventually crossed the equator and reached Cape St Augustine, which is at the latitude six degrees south. Here the coast turns south-south-west, and he abandoned his voyage further south because his ships became riddled with teredos.

Turning back, he retraced the same route as far as Trinidad and then north to Haiti. He then headed back to Spain, arriving in the summer of 1500 at the port of Santa Maria, where his friend de la Cosa was preparing his map. Vespucci did some writing and worked on his own maps. If de la Cosa and Vespucci did have access to Cabot's maps they would have put them to good use that summer. De la Cosa was preparing for his next exploration; he left port in October 1500 and returned to the area of Columbia in the Caribbean.[12]

Meanwhile, in Bristol, another expedition was preparing to leave for Brassyle. Two Bristol merchants teamed up with three Portuguese mariners from the Azores for a voyage to Greenland, the New Founde Lands and the sea to the north. Perhaps doubts were being expressed in Portugal that the mainland to the south and west of Brassyle was not Cathay, and that the way to the Orient may lie to the north-west. In March 1501 Thomas Ashhurst, John Thomas, Joao Fernandes, Francisco Fernandes and Joao Gonsalves sailed from Bristol. They explored the Greenland and Labrador coasts and made an attempt at finding a passage to Cathay. They returned to Bristol late that year, though Joao Fernandes died during the voyage.[13]

The following year, Hugh Elliot, a master with previous exploration experience, joined Fernandes, Ashhurst, and Thomas for yet another attempt. They returned to England with three natives, possibly Eskimos, who lived in London for several years.

Even at this time there was still no suggestion that the land that was attracting so much attention was a new continent. For the most part the English, the Portuguese and the Spanish still believed they were exploring peninsulas and islands generally in the proximity of Cathay and Indo-China. It was becoming clear, however, that the land next to the place they earlier called the Island of Brassyle was a landmass of considerable size.[14]

Ships that set sail from Bristol were still going to the same area that Bristol seamen had first visited some twenty years earlier and were even piloted by some of the same people involved in those earlier voyages. Similarly, the rutters issued to Elliot and other crews, as late as 1503, were derived from the same books that had been in use throughout these years.

In Bristol a group of merchants formed 'The Company of Adventurers to the New Founde Land' for the purpose of exploring and exploiting the area. However, the company is believed to have proved unprofitable and was dissolved after only a few years.

FIFTEEN

QUARTA ORBIS PARS

We may rightly call [it] a New World . . .
it transcends the view held by the ancients . . .
that there was no continent to the south
beyond the equator.
In those southern parts I have found a continent
more densely peopled and abounding in animals
than our Europe or Asia or Africa.

Mundus Novus, Amerigo Vespucci, August 1504.[1]

Vespucci sailed back to Spain in the summer of 1500. He immediately made plans to return to the New World and resume his search for the Cape of Catigara, the southernmost point of the Indo-Chinese peninsula, from where he would sail to India. He intended to travel down the east coast of what we now know as South America, starting at Cape St Augustine, the most southerly point he reached the previous year. He would be sailing along the coastline of land that the Pope had granted to Portugal, so he approached the royal family in Lisbon for sponsorship, which they granted.

He sailed from Lisbon on 14 May 1501, first to the Cape Verde Islands, located some 300 miles off the West African coast. He then sailed south-west across

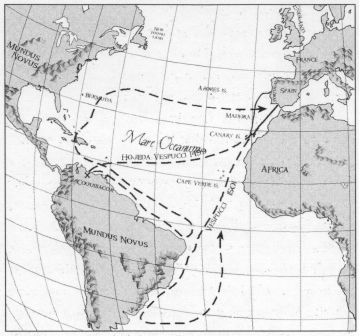

Vespucci's Voyages to the New World in 1499 and 1501. (*Courtesy of Jeff Reynolds*)

the Mare Oceanum to Cape St Augustine where he turned south. Several months later, in January 1502, he reached the site of present-day Rio de Janeiro and he continued south to a point a short distance past the mouth of the River Plate, which he is also credited with discovering. He charted the stars in the southern sky and attempted to determine the star that was situated over the South Pole. This was a remarkable scientific breakthrough for navigators sailing in the southern hemisphere.

Vespucci sailed nearly 3,000 miles along the new coast trying to reach the end of the peninsula before abandoning his search. He returned to Portugal via the island of South Georgia in the south Mare Oceanum, arriving in Lisbon in the summer of 1502.

It was during this, his 'third' voyage that he finally came to the realization that the new coast was neither part of Cathay nor of Indo-China but was, in fact, a fourth continent. This enlightened realization, together with his emerging techniques of measuring the globe, would fundamentally change the map of the world.

After his return to Portugal, he wrote a short book entitled *Mundus Novus* ('New World'), which was published in 1503. In this he described the plants and wildlife he saw along the coast and the native peoples he met. His book gained notoriety because of its lurid and promiscuous descriptions of the native women. In one incident, a sailor was seduced by a group of women and then killed. His flesh was cooked and eaten in full view of the ship. The crew was too frightened to intervene. *Mundus Novus* was a 'bestseller' and was published in fourteen editions and in several languages.

Vespucci had a long correspondence with Piero Soderini, a lifelong friend who was now the *Gonfaloniere*, or Head Magistrate, of Florence. He sent him detailed letters of his three voyages, the first being the 1497 crossing. One of these letters described his method of calculating longitude. He showed how he determined the earth's circumference and came to the conclusion that the new discoveries constituted a separate continent. These letters were published in at least ten editions.

He also wrote a series of long private letters to the Medici family, his former employer. In these letters he only describes two voyages, those of 1499 and 1501. It is this discrepancy that has contributed to the dispute as to whether Vespucci made the first voyage in 1497.

It was Vespucci himself who most likely sent copies of his published Soderini letters and probably his maps to the Duke of Lorraine, who in turn gave them to the young scholar, Matthias Ringmann. Like many other facets of this story, the Ringmann–Vespucci connection would have far-reaching consequences. The letters were written in Latin and were translated by Ringmann.

An edition of *The Three Voyages of Amerigo Vespucci*, which included a poem written by Ringmann, was published in Strasbourg in 1503. The three voyages described were those of 1497–8, 1499–1500 and 1501–2. Historians are very much divided in opinion about Vespucci's first voyage. Questions were raised soon after Vespucci's death by Sebastian Cabot, the son of John Cabot, and also by Columbus's biographer in *Historia de las Indias*. There is also evidence that Vespucci was in Seville in 1497. If Vespucci had sailed to South America in 1497, he, rather than Columbus, would have been the first European to set foot on the

American mainland. But his detractors say that more weight should be given to the private Medici letters than to the published Soderini letter.[2]

Vespucci may have made a second voyage bearing the Portuguese flag in 1503 under the command of Gonzalo Cuelho, with Juan de la Cosa navigating a second vessel. However, this voyage did not produce any discoveries of importance, and some doubt that Vespucci participated at all. In September 1504, after the return of this voyage, he sent more letters to his friend Soderini and his publication was updated. *The Four Voyages of Amerigo Vespucci* was also published in many editions and languages. This document would become the basis for a world map that was printed in St Dié, a remote village hidden away in the Franco-German borderland, far from either Lisbon or the Mare Oceanum.

In 1505 Vespucci was invited to Spain for private consultations where he was offered a high-ranking position with the Casa de Contratacion de las Indias (the Commercial House for the West Indies). He moved back to Spain, married Maria Cerezo, and was granted Spanish citizenship. In 1508 he was appointed Pilot Major, or Chief Navigator, of the state. In his capacity as the head of the Spanish Admiralty, he trained and granted licences to pilots, and he controlled the master map for the entire 'Fourth Continent'.

Portrait of Amerigo Vespucci: detail from
Waldseemüller's world map of 1507.
(*The British Library*)

Vespucci died in Seville in 1512 as a result of complications he developed from malaria, a disease he had contracted in the '*mundus novus*'.[3]

Vespucci has been discredited largely because of discrepancies between contemporary accounts of his various voyages. However, the fact that the Spanish government appointed him – a foreigner – to one of the most important positions in Spain is ample testament to his reputation and abilities. He was a brilliant scientist and was widely published. His intention to publish his map of the world, both as a flat map and as a globe, is evident from his writings to his employer; the Waldseemüller map may represent exactly what he had wanted to print himself.

The mass of information Vespucci collected between 1492 and 1503 would almost certainly have included sightings of the records from Cabot's 1497 voyage, de la Cosa's map drawn in 1500, and later maps produced in Spain and Portugal. We can only speculate about the maps and records from John Cabot's final voyage in 1498–9.

It is known that Cabot produced documents and maps that do not exist today. Given Amerike's prominence in 1497, his role as a merchant in the previous seventeen years and especially his association with the group that was actively trying to find Brassyle, the circumstantial evidence is sufficient to conclude that the name 'America' in all likelihood originated with Richard Amerike. Did Cabot use that name and did Vespucci transfer the name to his records? In the absence of surviving maps drawn by Vespucci we can only wonder as to the extent of the information provided to the cartographers at St Dié.

SIXTEEN

DISCOVERY OF A SPANISH FILING ERROR

Bristoll Arthurus Kemys et Ricardus ap Meryke Collectores Custumarum et
Subsidiorum Regis ibidem a festo Sci. Michaelis archangeli anno xiii Regis nunc
vsque idem festum Sci. Michaelis tunc proxime sequens, reddunt Computum de
mccccxxiiii. li. vii. s. x. d. q.
De quibus
Et in thesaurario in una tallia
pro Johanne Cabot xx. li

Customs Rolls, Bristol, 1499.[1]

There was very little interest in exploiting North America until well into the second half of the sixteenth century. Early settlements were proprietorships formed in England, which were granted royal charters with specific commercial endeavours in mind, such as growing tobacco, sugar or rice, or manufacturing maritime supplies like rope and pitchpine. An attempt to settle a colony on Roanoke Island in Virginia in 1585 failed, but in 1607 the first successful settlement at Jamestown, Virginia, was established primarily to supply tobacco to the English market. Richard Amerike had long since been forgotten, his heirs and descendants no longer carried his name, and his estate in Long Ashton had been recently absorbed by the wealthy Smythe family. However, a new generation of Bristolians were active in these colonial ventures. America existed as a wealthy and rapidly growing British colony for 170 years before the United States of America broke away after the revolutionary war in 1776. After a further conflict with Britain in 1812 stable trade and peaceful relations were established, relations which have continued to this day.

In 1892 the United States of America celebrated, in grand style, the 400th anniversary of Columbus's discovery of America. Five years later, in 1897, the authorities in the city of Bristol observed the 400th anniversary of Cabot's 1497 voyage in order to bring attention to his discovery of the North American mainland. They built a tower in the city, held lectures and staged special maritime events. These celebrations exposed earlier nineteenth-century research that had lain dormant for many years.

This revival of interest led to the publication of several books on the subject, and an immense amount of information about Cabot that had not come to light before was brought to the public's attention. Nothing was known up to that time of the fate of Cabot after he left Bristol on his second voyage (1498). Many people initially assumed he had returned to England but the complete lack of information available for the period

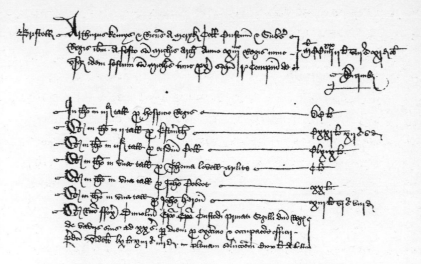

Customs Roll for Bristol, 1499. (*Dean and Chapter of Westminter*)

after 1498 led most historians to conclude that he had probably perished at sea.

In the 1890s Dr Edward Scott, keeper of the Muniments at Westminster Abbey, discovered a batch of Exchequer documents in the Abbey archives. Two of these ledgers were the customs and excise collections and expenditures for the City of Bristol for the years 1498 and 1499. Both recorded a payment to John Cabot of £20 for his pension. These documents caused some historians to believe that Cabot had returned to Bristol after his second expedition (1498). It now appears that his pension was paid to his wife. Dr Scott contacted a colleague in Bristol; the documents were then taken to Bristol to be examined further, and a short time later they were published.[2]

When the Bristol historian Alfred Hudd came across the documents he noticed that a name on each of them identifying one of the Customs Officers was uncannily close to the name 'America'. On one ledger the name was Richard Ameryk, and on the other, it was Richard ap Meryke. It transpired that Ameryk and ap Meryke were one and the same person.

Translated from the Latin, part of the document stated:

> Bristol.
> Arthur Kemys and Richard ap Meryke collectors of the King's customs and subsidies there, from Michaelmas in the 14th year of this King's Reign till the same feast next following,
> render their account of £1,424 7s 10 ¼d
> Out of which
> In the treasury in one tally
> in the name of John Cabot £20 0s 0d.

This discovery inspired further research about the man Amerike. He was linked with the brass plate on the tomb of John and Johanna Broke in St Mary Redcliffe Church and was identified as Johanna's father. His name also appeared in civic records in connection with his role as the King's Customs Officer and later as the Sheriff of Bristol. He was known to be a wealthy and active merchant and was almost certainly involved in the Fellowship of Merchants.

Arthur Kemys, the other name mentioned, was Amerike's assistant at the Customs House. He too came from a prominent local family. A rent ledger was discovered pointing to the fact that John Cabot's wife rented a house owned by Kemys for £2 a year.

These discoveries were enough for Hudd to conclude that Cabot may have named America after Richard Amerike. He first put forth his theory about the derivation of the name America from Richard Amerike to the Clifton Antiquarian Society in a lecture in 1908. The text of the lecture was published as a small booklet, which generated considerable interest, particularly in Bristol.

Since that time, significant new evidence has come to light showing Amerike's involvement in trade and his associations with the participants in the trading licence explorations in the years 1480 to 1483.

The first significant event was the discovery of a letter in 1955 in the Spanish National Archives. This accidental find had far-reaching implications for Bristol. It established that Bristol merchant ships had sailed to America considerably earlier than Columbus, something that had long been suspected but was difficult to prove.

Dr Hayward Keniston, a Romance language expert from the University of Michigan, had been undertaking research in letters in the Spanish National Archives in Simancas, in Spain. He discovered a letter written in Spanish to Christopher Columbus by Johan Day, a Bristol merchant. It was written between Christmas 1497 and March 1498 and contained a long report of the Cabot voyages of 1496 and 1497 and clearly formed part of a regular correspondence between Columbus and Day. Day stated:

> It is considered certain that the cape of the said land was found and discovered in the past by the men from Bristol who found 'Brazil' as your Lordship well knows. It was called the Island of Brazil, and it is assumed and believed to be the mainland that the men from Bristol found. [3]

Johan Day's letter to Columbus revealed that Columbus knew even before 1492 that Bristol merchants were sailing across the Atlantic to Brassyle. This letter also answered several questions that historians had been asking for several hundred years.

The Spanish language had a colloquial expression that alluded to a period of about twenty years. It was used in the letter, suggesting that the Bristol voyages to Brassyle were 'a generation' prior to 1497, when the letter was written. Day had claimed that: 'The said land was found and discovered "in the past" by the men from Bristol . . .' The English translation does not adequately convey this meaning, but given that Day was writing this in 1497, it gives credence to the first successful crossing being in 1480 or 1481. More importantly, when he wrote '. . . as your Lordship well knows' he provides the evidence that the Bristol merchants were sailing to the new founde land and that Columbus was aware of it.[4]

Day's letter states, as we have seen, that Cabot and the Bristol merchants saw fish drying on racks on the beaches, using exactly the same process that was developed in Iceland. He also mentions that Cabot attempted a crossing most likely the previous year, in 1496, but had to turn back 'because the crew was confusing him'. This earlier aborted voyage had not previously been known.[5]

Dr Keniston mentioned the letter to a colleague, Dr Louis Andre Vigneras, who immediately realized its importance. The letter had not been noticed before because of a simple clerical error. It had been filed with documents pertaining to English voyages to Brazil, when in fact it referred to Brassyle. The word 'Brazil' related to the vast tract of new land discovered south of the equator in the New World. It was named after the hard brazil wood that was found to flourish there. The voyage in question, however, referred to the mythical island that was purported to exist off the west coast of Ireland and was known by its Celtic name 'Brassyle'. The unearthing of this important letter introduced yet another character to the fifteenth-century stage.

Johan Day was a merchant who lived both in England and in Andalucia in southern Spain. He wrote the letter to Columbus while he was in the Spanish port of Santa Maria, near Cadiz.

This letter completely changed our understanding of the roles that Columbus, Cabot and the Bristol merchant traders played in the discovery of North America between 1480 and 1497, and gave a unique insight into what these individuals knew about each other. It removed much of the speculation about the existence of maps drawn by Cabot, where he landed in June 1497 and which part of the coastline he surveyed. It also stated that he gave names to many geographical features. Day even questioned Columbus's ethics in claiming the New World for Spain, knowing that the Bristol merchants had been there before him.

The most revealing piece of information is that Day said he would send a copy of Cabot's map to Christopher Columbus. This map was most likely in Columbus's hands within a few months of Cabot's voyage. If Day lived up to his promise, Columbus might just have received Cabot's map before he left on his third voyage the following May and Juan de la Cosa would have seen it before he produced his chart in 1500. Vespucci, who was sailing in the same fleet as his friend de la Cosa in 1499, also would have had access to it. If Juan de la Cosa and Amerigo Vespucci also saw Cabot's maps from his later 1498 expedition this might explain the five English flags and notation of 'the areas discovered by the English' that de la Cosa drew on his map. Speculation aside, the letter confirmed that Bristol merchants had played a much greater role in the discovery of North America than had previously been recognized.

John Balsall's ledgers, cargo manifests and trading records came to light in the 1960s in the archives of The Mercer Company in Bridgnorth in Shropshire. Balsall was the resident purser on board the *Trinity* on the trading voyage that left Bristol on 29 October 1480 for Spain and Portugal. Richard Amerike was the shipper of woollen cloth on this voyage in association with some of the participants who applied for the trading licence for 1480–3. These records were analysed and published in a paper by T.F. Reddaway and A.A. Ruddock in 1969. When combined and added to the extensive Port of Bristol customs records researched and published by E.M. Carus-Wilson in the 1930s, these seemingly mundane accounting records provided historians with a detailed record of the business dealings of many of the prominent merchants in Bristol.[6]

It became clear that Amerike not only was closely linked to Cabot's voyage in 1497 but that he was associated with the merchants who were granted the trading licence to search for Brassyle in 1480–3 some seventeen years earlier. His involvement with America would have pre-dated Columbus's discovery of the continent by twelve years. (Amerike was also identified as the shipper of two tuns of salt and corrupt wine to Ireland in 1480 on one of Thomas Croft's ships.)

This obscure figure, who was already known to have been Sheriff in 1501, now took on a new significance. His name also surfaced in the property deeds of three important landholdings: the Clifton Manor, Canynges Mansion on Redcliffe Street, and the Ashton-Phillips Estate.

Consequently, local historical documents took on a much greater importance. The annual civic records of the Bristol government had survived from the fifteenth and sixteenth centuries and were readily available for research purposes. There are two series of Kalendars in which local events were recorded by Bristol's town clerk. Ricart's Kalendar is the better known of the two. There are several examples from both series still in existence, though neither is complete. A summary of these Kalendars was made in 1565 by Maurice Toby, and in this compilation he uses the name America. This Kalendar record provides the most accurate dates for Cabot's successful voyage.

Under the mayoral year 1496–7, Toby recorded that John Drews was Mayor, Hugh Johnes was Sheriff, Thomas Vaughan and John Elyott were Bailiffs, and that:

This year [1497] on St John the Baptist's Day [June 24th], the land of America was found by the merchants of Bristowe, in a ship of Bristowe called the *Matthew*, the which said ship departed from the port of Bristowe the 2nd of May and came home again the 6th August following.[7]

His use of the term 'America' reveals a familiarity with the word, and it may have been used in the documents he had assembled and from which he was quoting, which were probably written much earlier. His Kalendar was a compilation of existing civic records and we can only speculate that his use of the name America indicates a level of acceptance over time, though there is no definitive evidence as to when or why.

The Toby manuscript, which was known and quoted from in the nineteenth century, is no longer in existence. It was owned and sold in the 1800s by the Fust family of Hill Court, Gloucestershire, and was eventually purchased by an antiquities dealer, Thomas Kerslake of Park Street, Bristol. Unfortunately in 1860 it was destroyed along with many other valuable manuscripts when his shop was engulfed in flames. Like all other aspects of the story of Richard Amerike, the missing pieces are tantalizing and intriguing.

SEVENTEEN

A MISSING PLAQUE

Paly of six, Or and Azure, on a fess Gules, three mullets Argent.

Richard Amerike's coat of arms[1]

Although Bristol is now a dynamic city of 400,000 people, it is still possible to explore here a medieval world that Richard Amerike would have recognized: Hoefnagle's map of 1580 can be used as the basis for a tour of the city centre today.

Bristol Bridge was the centre of Amerike's world. The fifteenth-century structure has long since disappeared, but the latest bridge crosses the River Avon at the same location and leads straight into the same narrow city streets. The plan of the city has hardly changed, and within a quarter of a mile are the banking area, the law courts, the old stock exchange building, and the markets. Amerike would still recognize the quays with their moorings, some sixteen churches, and the market area with its labyrinth of alleyways, cellar bars and eating houses.

To the north-east of the bridge is an entrance to the Castle. Oliver Cromwell ordered Bristol Castle to be disassembled, 170 years after Amerike's death.

Amerike's warehouses would have been on the quays along the River Avon, downstream from Bristol Bridge. Welsh Back, where the ships from South Wales docked, is still in use.

The house belonging to Arthur Kemys, which Cabot rented for his wife, stood on St Nicholas Street, which winds around behind the market from St Nicholas Church to Broad Quay. The shell of St Nicholas Church, where both Cabot and Columbus worshipped, stands near Bristol Bridge. A German incendiary bomb destroyed it in the blitz on 24 November 1940. The church has been partially rebuilt and serves as a civic building. Amerike's office in the Customs House looked out over the Broad Quay at the far end of St Nicholas Street.

On King Street, the pub and eating house called the Llandoger Trow has been in operation for 400 years. The buildings in 1500 would have looked very similar.

The sights on the half-mile walk from Bristol Bridge along Redcliffe Street to the magnificent St Mary Redcliffe Church are not very attractive. This area, known as Redcliffe, consisted of narrow and crowded streets of houses, artisan workshops and businesses. The river front was busy with shipping activity and warehouses. At about the halfway point and fronting the river is the site of Canynges's mansion, which Amerike acquired in settlement of a lawsuit. Some of the walls and a window from the original building have been incorporated into the new office development there.[2]

The church of St Mary Redcliffe can be seen from this vantage point. When Richard Amerike attended the funerals of William Canynges and John and Joan Jay here, the church was over 200 years old. Happier occasions would have been the wedding of Johanna to John Broke and the christenings of his grandchildren.

A carpet lies at the front of the choir just before the step up to the altar. Under the stone floor beneath this carpet, Johanna lies next to her husband, John Broke. The grave is marked by a brass plate that identifies her as Richard Amerike's daughter. A translation of the inscription reads:

> Here lies the body of that venerable man John Brook, sergeant at law of that most illustrious prince of happy memory King Henry the Eighth and Justice of Assize for the same King in the Western parts of England, and Chief Steward of the honourable house and monastery of the Blessed Mary of Glastonbury in the County of Somerset which John died on the 25th day of December in the year of Our Lord one thousand five hundred and 22. And near him rests Johanna his wife one of the daughters and heirs of Richard Amerike on whose souls may God have mercy. Amen.[3]

Beside this inscription is the grave of John Jay II, one of the owners of the *Trinity* who sailed to Lisbon so many years ago. He lies here with his wife, Joan, whose

Brass rubbing from the grave of John and Johanna Broke in St Mary Redcliffe Church, Bristol. (*Courtesy of Tim Tiley and St Mary Redcliffe, Medieval Monumental Brasses*)

brother, William Worcestre, wrote about his brother-in-law's attempts to find the Island of Brassyle. Also buried with them are their fourteen children, including John Jay III, who looked unsuccessfully for Brassyle in 1480. Likenesses of their six sons and eight daughters are shown on the plaque. The depiction of some of the daughters with their hair pinned up indicates they died unmarried.

William Canynges, the wealthy shipowner and politician, has his own large memorial in the church.

The whereabouts of Richard Amerike's grave is unknown. Given his standing in the community and his obvious associations with this church, it is hard to imagine that he is not buried in St Mary Redcliffe Church.

In the absence of standardized spelling conventions in his own lifetime, Richard Amerike's name was written many different ways. Sometimes it was ap Meric or ap Merryk. It appeared as Amerike in a land conveyance and on his daughter's grave. It showed up as Ameryk and Ap Meryke in the Westminster Abbey Customs Rolls. It was both Ameryke and Amyreke in the Balsall shipping accounts. The earlier spelling of ap Meric was reputedly the basis for the trademark that was used to identify his cargo.

Richard Amerike probably married his wife Lucy around 1460. They had two daughters, Johanna being the eldest. Nothing is known of Richard Amerike's other daughter. The only reference to her is the engraving on Johanna's grave, indicating there was another daughter and that she was an heir to his estate.

Nearly 200 years ago somebody pried loose and removed the brass of Amerike's coat of arms from Johanna's grave; the indent in the stone can still be seen. Local legend has it that it was taken to America, perhaps by a Merrick descendant, who wanted the crest of the 'daughter of America'. The description of the coat of arms on the missing brass in a nineteenth-century historical record of Bristol states:

> . . . in the chancel of St Mary Redcliffe [Broke's] brass remains, also until recently [probably early 1800s], the arms of Cobham and Brook, quarterly, with a crescent for difference, as well as Brook impaling Americk, viz – Paly of six, or, and az. on a fess gu. three mullets arg.

Johanna married John Broke in about 1486. He was from a politically powerful family in the Somerset town of Ilchester. Broke's grandfather, Thomas Broke, had been Lord Cobham. The title passed to the brother of John's father, who was the current Lord Cobham when John was born. Lord Cobham, Edmund (or Edward) Broke, was instrumental in King Edward IV's accession to the throne at the Battle of Mortimer's Cross on 3 February 1461, the same battle that was fought on the land belonging to the family of Thomas Croft, Amerike's predecessor at the Customs House.

William Shakespeare commemorates the Battle of Mortimer's Cross in his play *Henry VI, Part 3*, in which he depicts Cobham's role:

> You, Edward, shall to Edmund Brook Lord Cobham,
> With whom the Kentishmen will willingly rise:
> In them I trust, for they are soldiers,
> Witty, courteous, liberal, full of spirit.
>
> (Act I, Scene II, 11. 40–3)

Amerike gave the Clifton mansion to Johanna and John Broke. John Broke was a lawyer and Sergeant-at-Law to the royal court in London. Their eldest son, Thomas, was born in 1487. Richard Amerike spent his later years living on his Ashton-Phillips Estate, and his house still stands, in Yanley Lane, in the nearby village of Long Ashton.

Half a mile away from St Mary Redcliffe Church and across the city centre is Bristol cathedral, which Amerike would remember as St Augustine's Abbey. The cathedral fronts College Green, one of Bristol's many open spaces. Also adjacent to College Green is Bristol's city government building, the Council House. John Cabot's statue looks toward the city from the centre of the façade. The Lord Mayor's Chapel, a small church opposite the cathedral, is used exclusively by the Mayor and the city. This chapel houses the Poyntz family tombs and three of their heraldic shields

Richard Amerike's Coat of Arms.

incorporate Amerike's coat of arms.[4] The Merrick family, well established in the area around Sherborne in Dorset and Somerset in the 1500s were descended from the same family, attesting to this marriage connection. The Amerike crest is one-fourth of one crest, one-sixth of another, and one-tenth of the third.

Cabot Tower, built for the 1897 celebrations, is at the top of Brandon Hill behind the Council House. The Clifton Manor, of which Amerike owned one-third part, is about a quarter of a mile to the west of the tower.

It is unlikely that Amerike's crest (consisting of stars and stripes, in silver, red, gold and blue) had any influence on the design of Old Glory, the flag of the United States of America, though the similarities in design are uncanny. Amerike, after all, did precede the founding of the United States by nearly 300 years.

In colonial times, the American flag was the English Red Ensign, the flag of the merchant marine. This consisted of a red field, and in the top left quarter, the red cross of St George and the white diagonal cross of St Andrew on a blue background. On 1 January 1776, Washington flew his Grand Union flag over his revolutionary headquarters in Boston, Massachusetts. It was a modified Red Ensign, with six white horizontal stripes splitting the red field into seven red stripes. Washington's family coat of arms is similar to Amerike's and to this day it is the basis for the emblem of the city of Washington, D.C.

On 14 June 1777 the top left quarter, depicting the British flag, was replaced with a blue field with thirteen stars placed in a circle. The stars represented the new constellation of states, and the stripes the thirteen original colonies. Since that time the number of stars has been changed to represent the number of States in the Union.

However, even in the United States the origin of the flag's design is disputed. Congressman Francis Hopkinson claimed that he designed the flag. He was a signer of the Declaration of Independence and a member of the Continental Navy Board. In 1780 he sent the new government a bill demanding a small cask of wine for his troubles. [5]

During the 1700s, because of the extent of the shipping traffic and trade connections with colonial America, there were hundreds of Bristol sailors and merchants who were familiar with the eastern seaboard cities of Boston, New York, Philadelphia, Baltimore, Yorktown and Charles Town. [6] Bristolians settled in these cities and established businesses. Indeed, John Yeamans, Charles Town's founder and an early Governor of South Carolina, was a Bristolian, and Admiral Penn, the father of Pennsylvania's founder, is buried in St Mary Redcliffe Church. It is possible that the inspiration for the flag design was influenced by Amerike's coat of arms, which may have been known in the New World; but this does seem improbable.

The American Revolution in the 1770s caused upheaval in trade relations with the former mother country and for a while all ties were cut. However, after the peace settlement trade links were re-established and American ships started to visit Bristol again. Many of these sailors would have known St Nicholas Church (the sailors' church) and St Mary Redcliffe Church (the merchants' church) where Amerike's daughter is buried.

Most visitors to Bristol make a point of seeing the famous Clifton Suspension Bridge, which crosses the River Avon gorge, linking Clifton with the Ashton Estate. The bridge was constructed between 1830 and 1866 by the renowned nineteenth-century engineer, Isambard Kingdom Brunel. Postcards picture the River Avon at high tide when it is undoubtedly more attractive. A visitor seeing the river at both high and low tide will understand the significance of Columbus's recollections about Bristol's extreme tidal range.

However, the river level within the old city is no longer tidal. Two hundred years ago, a series of locks was constructed so that the water within the city harbour could be kept permanently at high tide. An artificial river channel called 'The Cut' now bypasses the original course of the river, paralleling it a few hundred yards to the south, which of course is tidal.

The headquarters of the Society of Merchant Venturers is located in Clifton. This organization obtained its charter in 1552 and many believe it evolved from the Fellowship of Merchants. Today its primary role is to administer merchant marine charities.

The *Matthew* still sails the waters in Bristol Harbour. A replica of the ship that transported Cabot to Brassyle was built at the end of the twentieth century and was sailed from Bristol to Newfoundland in 1997, re-creating Cabot's voyage exactly 500 years later. It is often moored about a mile downstream from St Mary Redcliffe Church next to SS *Great Britain*, the first of the modern propeller-driven iron-hulled ocean liners. The *Great Britain* was launched in 1842 and was also engineered by Brunel. It is undergoing restoration in the same dry dock where it was originally built. Both ships were built in Bristol's shipyards.

Today, when the *Matthew* is not sailing between the coastal towns of south-west England, it carries visitors on scenic tours on the River Avon within the city of Bristol. One can easily imagine that there are barrels of salt, corrupt wine, leather hides, small pigs, several chickens, and enough food, beer, and firewood for several months below deck in the hold. The fire is alight in the galley on the deck, where the meals are cooked.

With the falling tide beneath the bluffs of Clifton, the *Matthew* sails to the mouth of the Avon and out into the current. The full sails are raised and fresh wind takes the ship out into the Bristol Channel and to the rough seas of the Mare Oceanum toward a distant small fishing village on the Island of Brassyle, which is now called America.

APPENDIX A

Dispatch of Pedros de Ayala, Spanish Ambassador to London, 25 July 1498.

I think your Highnesses have already heard how the King of England [Henry VII] has equipped a fleet to explore certain islands or mainland which he has been assured certain persons who set out last year from Bristol in search of the same have discovered. I have seen the map made by the discoverer [Cabot], who is another Genoese like Columbus, who has been in Seville and at Lisbon seeking to obtain persons to aid him in this discovery. For the last seven years the people of Bristol have equipped two, three and four caravels to go in search of the islands of Brazil and Seven Cities according to the fancy of this Genoese. The king made up his mind to send thither, because last year sure proof was brought him they had found land. The fleet he prepared, which consisted of five vessels, was provisioned for a year. News has come that one of these, in which sailed another, Friar Buil [who sailed with Columbus in his second voyage], has made land in Ireland in a great storm with the ship badly damaged.

The Genoese kept on his way. Having seen the course they are steering and the length of the voyage, I found that what they have discovered or are in search of is possessed by Your Highnesses because it is at the cape which fell to Your Highnesses by the convention with Portugal [Treaty of Tordesillas, 1494]. It is hoped they will be back by September. I will let Your Highnesses know about it. The king has spoken to me several times on the subject. He hopes the affair may turn out profitable. I believe the distance is not 400 leagues. I told him I believed the islands were those found by Your Highnesses, and although I gave him the main reason, he would not have it. Since I believe Your Highnesses will already have notice of all this and also of the chart or mappemonde which this man has made, I do not send it now, although it is here, and so far as I can see exceedingly false, in order to make believe that these are not part of the said islands (of Your Highnesses).

Reproduced from H.P. Biggar, *Precursors*, 1911.

APPENDIX B

Translation of Johan Day's letter to Columbus, the Lord Grand Admiral.

Your Lordship's servant brought me your letter. I have seen its contents and would be most desirous and most happy to serve you. I do not find the book Inventio Fortunada and I thought that he was bringing it with my things, and I am very sorry not to find it because I wanted very much to serve you. I am sending another book of Marco Polo and a copy [map] of the land which has been found. I do not send the map because I am not satisfied with it for the many occupations forced me to make it in a hurry at the time of my departure; but from the said copy your Lordship will learn what you wish to know: for in it are named the capes of the mainland and the islands, and thus you will see where the land was first sighted, since most of the land was discovered after turning back.

Thus your Lordship will know that the cape nearest to Ireland is 1,800 miles west of Dursey Head which is in Ireland, and the southernmost part of the Island of Seven Cities [Newfoundland?] is west of Bordeaux River, and your Lordship will know that he landed at only one spot of the mainland, near the place where land was first sighted; and they disembarked there with a crucifix and raised banners and the arms of the Holy Father; and those of the King of England, my master, and they found tall trees of the kind masts are made, and other smaller trees, and the country is very rich in grass.

In that particular spot, as I told your Lordship, they found a trail that went inland, they saw a site where a fire had been made, and they saw manure of animals which they thought to be farm animals, and they saw a stick half a yard long pierced at both ends, carved and painted with brazil, and by such signs they believe the land to be inhabited. Since he was with just a few people, he did not dare advance inland beyond the shooting distance of a cross-bow, and after taking in fresh water he returned to his ship.

All along the coast they found many fish like those which in Iceland are dried in the open and sold in England and other countries, and these fish are called in English 'stockfish': and thus following the shore they saw two forms running on land one after the other; but they could not tell if they were human beings or animals; and it seemed to them that there were fields where they thought might also be villages, and they saw a forest whose foliage looked beautiful.

They left England toward the end of May, and must have been on the way 35 days before sighting land; the wind was east-north-east and the sea calm going and coming back, except for one day when he ran into a storm two or three days before finding land; and going so far out his compass needle failed to point north and marked two rhumbs below. They spent about one month discovering the coast and from the above mentioned cape of the mainland which is nearest to Ireland, they returned to the coast of Europe in fifteen days. They had the wind behind them, and he reached Brittany because the sailors confused him, saying that he was heading too far north. From there he came to

Bristol, and he went to see the King to report to him all of the above mentioned; and the King granted him a pension of twenty pounds sterling to sustain himself until the time comes when more will be known of this business, since with God's help it is hoped to push through plans for exploring the said land more thoroughly next year with ten or twelve vessels – because in his voyage he had only one ship of 50 'toneles' and twenty men and food for seven or eight months – and they want to carry out this new project.

It is considered certain that the cape of the said land was found and discovered in the past by the men from Bristol who found 'Brazil' as your Lordship well knows. It was called the Island of Brazil, and it is assumed and believed to be the mainland that the men from Bristol found.

Since your Lordship wants information relating to the first voyage, here is what happened: he went with one ship, his crew confused him, he was short of supplies and he ran into bad weather, and he decided to turn back.

Magnificent Lord, as to other things pertaining to the case, I would like to serve your Lordship if I were not prevented in doing so by the occupations of great importance relating to shipments and deeds for England which must be attended to at once and keep me from serving you, but rest assured Magnificent Lord, of my desire and natural intention to serve you, and when I find myself in other circumstances and more at leisure, I will take pains to do so; and when I get news from England about the matters referred to above – for I am sure that everything has to come to my knowledge – I will inform your Lordship of all that would not be prejudicial to the King my master. In payment of some services which I hope to render you, I beg your Lordship to kindly write me about such matters, because the favour you will thus do me will greatly stimulate my memory to serve you in all the things that may come to my knowledge. May God keep prospering your Lordship's magnificent state according to your merits. Whenever your Lordship should find it convenient, please remit the book or order it to be given to Master George.

I kiss your Lordship's hands
Johan Day

> Translated by Dr Louis Vigneras, 1956,
> Williamson, *The Cabot Voyages*, 1962.

APPENDIX C

Letters of John Cabot's Voyages.

Letter from Lorenzo Pasqualigo to his brothers Alvise and Francesco, London, 23 August 1497.

Our Venetian, who went with a small ship from Bristol to find new islands, has come back, and says he has discovered, 700 leagues off, the mainland of the country of the Gran Cam, and that he coasted along it for 300 leagues, and landed, but did not see any person. But he has brought here to the king certain snares spread to take game, and a needle for making nets, and he found some notched trees, from which he judged that there were inhabitants. Being in doubt, he came back to the ship. He has been away three months on the voyage, which is certain, and, in returning, he saw two islands to the right, but he did not wish to land, lest he should lose time for he was in want of provisions. This king has been much pleased. He says that the tides are slack, and do not make currents as they do here. The king has promised for another time, ten armed ships as he desires, and has given him all the prisoners, except such as are confined for high treason, to go with him, as he has requested; and has granted him money to amuse himself till then. Meanwhile, he is with his Venetian wife and his sons at Bristol. His name is Zuam Talbot, and he is called the Great Admiral, great honour being paid to him, and he goes dressed in silk. The English are ready to go with him, and so are many of our rascals. The discoverer of these things has planted a large cross in the ground with a banner of England, and one of St. Mark, as he is a Venetian; so that our flag has been hoisted very far away.

Extract from the first dispatch of Raimondo di Soncino to the Duke of Milan, 24 August 1497.

Some month afterwards His Majesty sent a Venetian, who is a distinguished sailor, and who was much skilled in the discovery of new islands, and he has returned safe, and has discovered two very large and fertile islands, having, it would seem, discovered the seven cities 400 leagues from England to the westward. These successes led His Majesty at once to entertain the intention of sending him with fifteen or twenty vessels.

Second dispatch of Raimondo di Soncino to the Duke of Milan, 18 December 1497.

My most illustrious and most excellent Lord,

Perhaps amidst so many occupations of your Excellency it will not be unwelcome to learn how this Majesty has acquired a part of Asia without drawing his sword. In this kingdom there is a certain Venetian named Zoanne Caboto, of gentle disposition, very expert in navigation, who, seeing that the most serene Kings of Portugal and Spain had occupied unknown islands, meditated the achievement of a similar acquisition for the said Majesty. Having obtained royal privileges securing to himself the use of the dominions he might discover, the sovereignty being reserved to the Crown, he entrusted his fortune to a small vessel with a crew of 18 persons, and set out from Bristo, a port in the western part of this kingdom. Having passed Ibernia, which is still further to the west, and then shaped a northerly course, he began to navigate to the eastern part, leaving the North Star on the right hand; and having wandered thus for a long time, at length he hit upon land, where he hoisted the royal standard, and took possession for his Highness, and, having obtained various proofs of his discovery, he returned. The said Messer Zoanne, being a foreigner and poor, would not have been believed if the crew, who are nearly all English, and belonging to Bristo, had not testified that what he said was the truth. This Messer Zoanne has the description of the world on a chart, and also on a solid sphere which he has constructed, and on which he shows where he has been; and, proceeding towards the east, he has passed as far as the country of the Tanais. And they say that there the land is excellent and [the climate?] temperate, suggesting that brasil and silk grow there. They affirm that the sea is full of fish, which are not only taken with a net, but also with a basket, a stone being fastened to it in order to keep it in the water; and this I have heard stated by the said Messer Zoanne.

The said Englishmen, his companions, say that they took so many fish that this kingdom will no longer have need of Iceland, from which country there is an immense trade in the fish they call stock-fish. But Messer Zoanne has set his mind on higher things, for he thinks that, when that place has been occupied, he will keep on still further towards the east, where he will be opposite to an island called Cipango, situated in the equinoctial region, where he believes that all the spices of the world, as well as the jewels, are found. He further says that he was once at Mecca, whither the spices are brought by caravans from distant countries; and having inquired from whence they were brought and where they grow, they answered that they did not know, but that such merchandise was brought from distant countries by other caravans to their home; and they further say that they are also conveyed from other remote regions. And he adduced this argument, that if the eastern people tell those in the south that these things come from a far distance from them, presupposing the rotundity of the earth, it must be that the last turn would be by the north towards the west; and it is said that in this way the route would not cost more than it costs now, and I also believe it. And what is more, this Majesty, who is wise and not prodigal, reposes such trust in him because of what he has already achieved, that he gives him a good maintenance, as Messer Zoanne has himself told me. And it is said that before long his Majesty will arm some ships for him, and will give him all the malefactors to go to that country and form a colony, so that they hope to establish a greater depot of spices in London than there is in Alexandria. The principal people in the enterprise belong to Bristo. They are great seamen, and, now that they know where to go, they say that the voyage thither will not occupy more than 15 days after leaving Ibernia. I have also spoken with a Burgundian, who was a companion of Messer Zoanne, who affirms all this, and who wishes to return because the Admiral (for so Messer Zoanne is entitled) has given him an island, and has given another to his barber of Castione, who is a Genoese, and both look upon themselves as Counts; nor do they look upon my Lord the Admiral as less than a Prince. I also believe that some poor Italian friars are going on this voyage, who have all had bishoprics promised to them. And if I had made friends with the Admiral when he was about to sail, I should have got an archbishopric at least; but I have thought that the benefits reserved for me by your Excellency will be more secure. I would venture to pray that, in the event of a vacancy taking place in my absence, I may be put in possession, and that I may not be superseded by those who, being present, can be more diligent than I, who am reduced in this country to eating at each meal ten or twelve kinds of victuals, and to being three hours at table every day, two for love of your Excellency, to whom I humbly recommend myself.

London, 18 Dec. 1497, your Excellency's most humble servant, Raimundus.

The text of these letters is from the Hakluyt Society's edition of Columbus's *Journal*. This text is provided by the Internet Modern History Sourcebook.

APPENDIX D

Bristol Evening Post, Friday 30 April 1943.

Ameryk and America

Although we like to think that Cabot discovered America – and there seems historical evidence in support of the fact – most Americans seem to favour Columbus' claim.

I was not a little surprised therefore, to hear Gen. H.R. Ingles, presenting the Stars and Stripes to the Lord Mayor, say: 'Cabot was really the discoverer of what is now known as America.'

Concerning that statement, I have to thank Mr H.R. Simpson (MA, Camb.) for an interesting contribution.

We Gave Her Name

'I think you could assure Americans that they owe not only their name, but their flag to Bristol', he writes. 'The accepted derivation of the word America from

Amerigo Vespucci is based on evidence so slight as to be almost fantastic. The name America was given by Richard Ameryk, Lord of the Manor of Clifton, and sometime Sheriff and Receiver of the King's Customs at Bristol.

Ameryk, from his connection with Canynge (his sister seems to have been that worthy's mistress), undoubtedly shared the common Bristol interest in discovery: it is even possible that he held a patent [trading licence] from Edward IV giving him a title to anything that could be found in the West.'

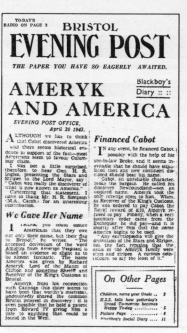

'Ameryk and America', *The Evening Post.*

Financed Cabot

In any event, he financed Cabot, possibly with the help of his son-in-law, Brooke, and it seems inevitable that he should have stipulated that any new continent disclosed should bear his name.

Cabot, an unreliable character, broke the bargain. He called his discovery Newfoundland – not an inspired name. Ameryk took the only revenge open to him. When as Receiver of the King's Customs, he was ordered to pay Cabot the Royal reward of £10, Ameryk refused to pay. Finally, when a very summary order came from the Exchequer, he did pay – and it is shortly after that that the name America begins to be used.

Any encyclopaedia will give the derivation of the Stars and Stripes, but the fact remains that the arms of the Ameryk family were stars and stripes. A curious coincidence, to say the least of it.

CAST OF CHARACTERS

Dates of birth and death are given where known.

Amerike, Lucy   Wife of Richard Amerike.

Amerike, Richard   (also ap Meryk, Richard) *c.* 1440–1503. Wealthy landowner and merchant who traded with Spain and Portugal. He was one of the chief financial backers of the fishing expeditions to Brassyle, beginning in the 1470s, and provided financial assistance for Cabot's expeditions to the New World on the *Matthew*. He was appointed as the King's Customs Officer in Bristol in 1486.

ap Meurig, Hywel   *c.* 1270–1330. Welsh prince from the Brecon area, related to the Clanvows and bearing the same coat of arms as Richard Amerike.

Balsall, John   Resident purser on board the *Trinity* in the late 1470s.

Behaim, Martin   1459–1507. German cartographer and navigator. Behaim produced a globe in 1490 based on Toscanelli's map.

Broke, Arthur   Son of Johanna and John Broke.

Broke, David   1489–1558. Second son of Johanna and John Broke.

Broke, Hugh   *c.* 1515–88. Son and heir of Thomas Broke.

Broke, Joan   Daughter of Johanna and John Broke.

Broke, Johanna   *c.* 1462–1538. Daughter of Richard Amerike. Her remains are buried in St Mary Redcliffe Church.

Broke, John	*c.* 1455–1522. Husband of Johanna Amerike Broke and grandson of Lord Cobham and Sergeant-at-Law to the court in London.
Broke, Thomas	1487–1537. Eldest son of Johanna and John Broke.
Cabot, John	1450–99. Celebrated navigator and explorer, who discovered the American mainland. Cabot gained sponsorship from the Crown to explore a northern passage to China. He sailed on a Bristol ship called the *Matthew*.
Cabot, Ludovico	Son of John Cabot.
Cabot, Sancius	*c.* 1480–99. Son of John Cabot. He accompanied his father on a voyage to the New World in 1498.
Cabot, Sebastian	1476–1557. Son of John Cabot.
Cantino, Alberto	Italian diplomat in Lisbon who illegally obtained a Portuguese map of the New World and smuggled it to his employer, the Duke of Ferrara, Ercole d'Este.
Canynges, Thomas	Nephew of William Canynges. He was kidnapped by pirates and held for ransom.
Canynges, William	1399–1474. Wealthy merchant and owner of the Canynges Company, which possessed the largest fleet of ships in Bristol in the late fifteenth century and controlled all fish trade with Iceland. Canynges was Mayor and Member of Parliament for Bristol.
Clanvow, Elizabeth	Wife of Sir John Poyntz. They married in 1343.
Columbus, Bartholomew	1461–1515. Brother of Christopher Columbus. He and Christopher worked as chart makers and merchants together in Lisbon.
Columbus, Christopher	1451–1506. Renowned discoverer of the Caribbean Islands, Cuba and Santo Domingo.
Columbus, Diego	1480–1526. Son of Christopher Columbus.
Columbus, Fernando	1488–1539. Illegitimate son of Christopher Columbus who wrote an account of his father's life.

Croft, Thomas	1435–88. The King's Customs Officer in Bristol prior to 1485 and Member of Parliament for Leominster, Herefordshire. He was named on the trading licence for the years 1480–3 and was also a part-owner of the *Trinity*.
Day, Johan	Bristol merchant who wrote to Columbus about the voyages of the Bristol merchants and of John Cabot. He had lived in southern Spain and may have worked for Spanish interests.
de Arana, Dona Beatriz Enriquez	Mistress of Christopher Columbus.
de Ayala, Pedros	Spanish envoy in London in 1497.
de Balboa, Vasco	1475–1517. Spanish conquistador and explorer.
Nunez	Balboa was the first European to sight the eastern shore of the Pacific Ocean.
de la Cosa, Juan	1450–1509. Cartographer who explored and charted maps of the east coast of the New World. He sailed and owned the *Santa Maria* in Columbus's first expedition in 1492.
de la Fount, William	*c.* 1430–96. Bristol merchant who traded with Iceland as well as Spain and Portugal. He was named on the trading licence for the years 1480–3.
de Las Casas, Father Bartholomeo	Bishop of Chiapaz in 1559. Columbus's biographer.
de Peranza, Dona Ines	Daughter of Christopher Columbus's mistress.
de Sandancourt, Jean Basin	Member of the Gymnasium Vosgense.
di Soncino, Raimondo	Milan's representative in London in 1496 and a friend of John Cabot.

Elliot, Hugh	Born *c*. 1460. Captain of at least two voyages to Brassyle. Sheriff of Bristol in 1501.
Gutenberg, Johan	1394–1468. Inventor of the printing press.
Hojeda, Admiral Alonzo	1470–1515. Spanish admiral known for his cruel and ruthless behaviour. He made voyages to the New World, joining Columbus in the Caribbean. The Spanish Crown rewarded him for his patriotic work in stopping English encroachment from the north.
Island, Willelmus	Icelandic national who lived in Bristol and later became an English subject. As a merchant he specialized in the Portuguese market.
Jay, Henry	Son of John Jay I. Upon his father's death, his shares in the Bristol ships passed to him and his brother, John Jay II.
Jay, Joan	*c*. 1425–90. Wife of John Jay II.
Jay, John, I	*c*. 1395–1468. Influential Bristol merchant who was part-owner of the *Trinity*. Jay owned several ships and had business interests in many others.
Jay, John, II	*c*. 1420–80. Son of John Jay I. Upon his father's death, his shares in the Bristol ships passed to him and his brother, Henry.
Jay, John, III	Born *c*. 1450. Grandson of John Jay I. He was on board the vessel that searched for Brassyle in 1480 and was the Sheriff of Bristol in 1499.
Kemys, Arthur	Amerike's assistant at the Customs House. Cabot rented a house for his wife from Kemys.
King Joao II	King of Portugal 1481–95.
King Manuel I	King of Portugal 1495–1521.

Cast of Characters

Lloyd	The 'most skilful mariner in England' in 1480. It is believed that he skippered a voyage on the *Trinity* that took a clandestine detour to look for the Island of Brassyle.
Lud, Gautier	Secretary to Duke Rene and a member of the Gymnasium Vosgense. Lud owned a printing press.
Lud, Nicholas	Nephew of Gautier Lud and a member of the Gymnasium Vosgense.
Marchena, Friar Antonio	Friar who lived at la Rabida Monastery in Huelva, Spain. He was an expert in astronomy, astrology, and cosmography.
Martinez, Canon Fernao	Canon of Lisbon cathedral in 1474.
Mercator, Gerard	1512–94. Cartographer who published a world map in the city of Duisberg in the Duchy of Cleves in 1538. This map named North and South America.
Perestrella, Felipa Monez	Wife of Christopher Columbus. She was the aristocratic daughter of an Italian diplomat who lived in Lisbon with his Portuguese wife.
Perez, Abbot Juan	Abbot of la Rabida Monastery in Huelva, Spain, and one of Columbus's strongest advocates. Diego Columbus lived at this monastery.
Polo, Marco	1254–1324. Venetian traveller and explorer. Polo was the first European to cross the entire continent of Asia and leave a record of what he saw and heard.
Poyntz, Sir John	The wealthiest and most politically powerful person in Bristol in the mid-1300s.
Ptolemy	87–150 BC. Astronomer, mathematician, and geographer who considered the earth to be the centre of the universe.

Queen Isabella I	1451–1501. Queen of Spain 1474–1501; wife of King Ferdinand V (1452–1516), who backed Christopher Columbus's expeditions to find a passage to India.
Rene, Duke	1451–1508. Duke of Lorraine who, in order to produce a world map, retained Waldseemüller. The Duke and the Canon of St Dié formed an intellectual group known as the Gymnasium Vosgense in 1500 to widen knowledge of cosmography and geometry.
Ringmann, Matthias	1482–1511. Poet and teacher of Latin and Greek and a member of the Gymnasium Vosgense.
Soderini, Piero	1454–?. Lifelong friend of Vespucci and the Head Magistrate of Florence during Vespucci's expeditions.
Spencer, William	1420–95. Mayor of Bristol 1474 and 1479 and Member of Parliament. He was granted a trading licence for the years 1480–3.
Straunge, Robert	1435–?. Mayor of Bristol 1475, 1482 and 1489 and Member of Parliament on two occasions. He was granted a trading licence.
Sturmy, Robert	Wealthy Bristol merchant who gave his residence to the city to be used as the Cloth Hall. A portion of the building was used by the Fellowship of Merchants.
Thorne, Nicholas	Brother of Robert Thorne.
Thorne, Nicholas	c. 1494–1550. Son of Robert Thorne.
Thorne, Robert	c. 1460–1519. Sailed with Hugh Elliott to Brassyle.
Thorne, Robert, the Younger	1492–1532. Son of Robert Thorne.
Toscanelli, Paolo del Pozzo	1397–1482. Brilliant mathematician, astronomer, and cosmographer who produced a map showing

that India could be reached by sailing west across
the Atlantic Ocean.

Vespucci, Amerigo 1454–1512. Italian discoverer who initially
voyaged to the New World under the Spanish flag.
Vespucci realized that the New World was a fourth
continent. With his background in astronomy, he
calculated the circumference of the earth at the
equator within an accuracy of 50 miles.

Waldseemüller, 1470–1519. Accomplished cosmographer and
Martin cartographer who published a revolutionary world
map in 1507.

Worcestre, William c. 1415–85. Prolific writer on Bristol's history. He
was the brother of Joan Jay.

English Monarchs 1421–1547

King Henry VI 1421–71 (reigned 1422–61).
King Edward IV 1442–83 (reigned 1461–70).
King Edward V 1470–83 (reigned 1483:
uncrowned).
King Richard III 1452–85 (reigned 1483–5).
King Henry VII 1457–85 (reigned 1485–1509).
King Henry VIII 1491–1547 (reigned 1509–47).

GLOSSARY

£ s d   Pounds, shillings and pence. In the 1400s, a good wage for a skilled shipwright was 6d a day or £7 a year. By this measure Amerike's annual salary of £6 13s 4d was the equivalent of an artisan's wage, and Cabot's annual pension of £20 was three years' wages. The *Trinity*'s cost of £1,200 is the equivalent of about £360,000 in today's money.

ANTILLIA   Another name for the Island of Seven Cities.

AZURE   A heraldic term for blue.

BASQUES   The inhabitants of the area roughly between Bayonne in France and Bilboa in Spain. These fiercely independent people are descended from eastern Mediterranean bloodlines.

BRASSYLE   (also Brasyle, Brasil, Hi-Brassyle, Brazil). An island thought to be located about 400 miles west of Ireland. It has no connection to present-day Brazil in South America.

BRAZIL WOOD A hard wood from which a red dye was made.

BRETONS   Inhabitants of Brittany in north-west France. Brittany was once an independent country.

BROADCLOTH Woollen cloth 24 yards long by 2 yards wide. It was used to make expensive suits.

BUSHEL   8 gallons.

CARTOUCHE An ornate or ornamental frame.

CATHAY	China.
CATIGARA	also Vietnam, Indo-China (Cape of Catigara: Singapore)
CHIPANGA	Japan.
CLOTH	Woollen cloth twenty-four yards long by one yard wide.
CORRUPT WINE	Vinegar.
COSMOGRAPHY	The study of astronomy, the world, and the cosmos.
COSMOLOGY	A branch of astronomy dealing with the origin and structure of the universe.
CWT	A hundredweight, 112 pounds, one-twentieth of a tun.
DENIZEN	A foreigner who is granted rights in his adopted country, similar to a working visa.
FESS	A heraldic term that means located at the mid-point of the crest.
FESTOON	An ornamental representation of a decorative chain.
GORE	A map projection that can be cut out and shaped into a globe.
GRAND BANKS	The shallow waters off the south-eastern coast of Newfoundland. They were once the best fishing grounds in the world.
GULES	A heraldic term for red.
ISLAND OF SEVEN CITIES	A large island thought to be located about 1,000 miles west of Portugal.
KRILL	Minute shrimp that populate the cold northern waters and are eaten by fish.
LAST	640 gallons.

Glossary

MARE OCEANUM The Atlantic Ocean. This name, given by Marco Polo, was used until the late sixteenth century.

MULLET A heraldic term for stars on a coat of arms.

OR A heraldic term for gold.

PALY A heraldic term for vertical stripes on a coat of arms.

RUTTERS Detailed sailing instructions that were handwritten in a pocket-sized book. The word comes from the French *routier* or route book. Rutters were available for most coastlines and major port-to-port destinations within Europe. They provided directions from landmark to landmark, including the bearing and distance from the previous landmark and any information relating to harbours, estuaries, depth soundings, winds, currents, sea kelp, and bird life. Fires that were maintained on headlands and hills were identified. The 100-fathom (600-foot) depth contour was also included. Rutters were given to the captain of a ship with the itinerary and sailing papers. They were used until the early sixteenth century. Printed rutters later became available

SALT COD Cod fish that has been filleted compressed and packed between layers of salt.

STOCKFISH Air-dried cod fish that has been filleted.

STOCKS Wooden racks from which cod fish were hung to dry.

SUBSIDY Duty payable on imported goods.

TEREDOS A tropical shipworm.

TRADING LICENCE An internationally recognized document issued by a government that authorizes the holder to explore and trade within the terms of the document.

TUN OR TUNNE   A 252-gallon cask or barrel. When full of wine, it weighed approximately 2,500 lbs. Tun was also used as the unit of measurement for the carrying capacity of a ship.

WOAD   A cloth dye made from burnt wood. It was imported and used in vast quantities.

NOTES

Preface

1   Quoted in James Wilson, *St Mary Redcliffe* (booklet).

One

1   Father Bartholomeo de las Casas, *Historia Generale de las Indies*, 1559, Bell Library, University of Minnesota website.
2   Catholic Encyclopedia website (article on Waldseemüller by Jos. Fischer).
3   Ibid.
4   Catholic Encyclopedia website (article on Vespucci by Gustavo Uzielli).
5   Bell Library, University of Minnesota website.
6   Lloyd Brown, *The Story of Maps*, Dover Publications, 1977, pp. 156–8.
7   Waldseemüller's world map of 1507, the *Cosmographiæ Introductio, Description of the World* and *The Four Voyages of Amerigo Vespucci*, United States Catholic Historical Society, 1907.
8   To give away state secrets from the map depository in Portugal carried the death penalty.
9   Ian Wilson, *The Columbus Myth*, Simon and Schuster 1991, p. 118.
10 Waldseemüller *Description of the World* and the *Cosmographiæ Introductio*.
11 Waldseemüller, *Cosmographiae Introductio*, Cartographic Images website, slide 312.

12   Richard Hakluyt, *Principall Navigation*, 1589.

13   De las Casas, *Historia Generale de las Indies*, 1559.

14   Daniel Boorstin, *The Discoverers*, New York, 1983, p. 252.

15   Library of Congress Press Release. In addition to the main 1507 map the Prince Waldburg-Wolfegg has offered to sell for $4,000,000 the rare sea chart known as the Carta Marina, also drawn by Waldseemüller, and two incomplete sets of celestial gores. The Carta Marina was based on unpublished nautical charts kept secret by explorers. It is the first printed nautical chart of the modern world. The borders are decorated, and the map is alive with cartouches, festoons, and ornate illustrations. It includes a drawing of an exotic opossum in South America and a rhinoceros in Africa.

16   Alfred Hudd lecture, Bristol 1908, published 1910.

Two

1   Cartographic Images website, slide 252.

2   F.H.M. Prescott, *Once to Sinai*, Macmillan Co., 1958 (quoted in American Spice Trade Association website).

3   Marco Polo's *Description of the World*, *National Geographic Magazine*, May/June/July 2001.

Three

1   Fernando Colon, trans. Benjamin Keen, *The Life of Admiral Christopher Columbus by his Son*, New Brunswick Rutgers University Press, New Jersey, 1959 (quoted in *Christopher Columbus, the Age of Exploration, an Encyclopedia*, ed. Silvio A. Bedini, Da Capo 1998, article by Rebecca Catz, p. 175.

2   John Dyson and Peter Christopher, *Columbus for Gold, God and Glory*, Simon and Schuster/Madison Press, 1991, pp. 48–54.

3   *Christopher Columbus, the Age of Exploration, an Encyclopedia*, article by David Quinn, p. 85; Helen Nader, p. 171; Rebecca Catz, p. 175; Einer Haugen, p. 314; Helga Ingstad, p. 690.

4 Colon, trans. Keen, *The Life of Admiral Christopher Columbus*. The theory that Columbus visited Bristol and sailed to Iceland on a Bristol ship is based solely on the writings of Christopher Columbus's son Fernando (or Hernando) Colon. He wrote *The Life of Admiral Christopher Columbus by his Son*, from his father's notes after his death. No specific details of the voyage exist, but he tells us it did originate in Bristol. He speaks of the extreme tidal range, which he could only have observed in Bristol. He makes reference to Iceland, where the Bristol ships traded. He also mentions Galway in Ireland. The tidal variations in the Mediterranean Sea are minimal, never rising more than a few feet. The same applies to the Atlantic Ocean and Iceland. However, the sea between England and South Wales and the approach to Bristol has an extremely high tidal variation that can be as great as 50 feet in March and September. This is a major problem for shipping. Bristol's location is unique in Europe in that it is situated at the narrow end of a long funnel formed by the Bristol Channel, the estuary of the River Severn, and the River Avon. As the tide turns, the waters surge into the funnel and flood the city's port, and the harbour is drained equally rapidly as the tide recedes. In Columbus's day, Bristol would have been the only location where a phenomenon such as this could have been observed. The only other places in the world that experience such extreme tidal variations are outside Europe. They include the Bay of Fundy in Canada, an estuary in China, and the Cook Inlet in Alaska, all of which have a similar geographical configuration.

5 William Worcestre, 1480 (quoted in William Barrett, *History and Antiquities of the City of Bristol*, 1789). The Canynges Company traded almost exclusively in the northern markets in the Baltic Sea and Scandinavia, and was the major Bristol-based shipping business. It was also the largest business in the city, owning a fleet of ten merchant ships. The *Mary Redcliffe* had a 500-tun capacity, and the *Mary and John*, which was sailing in the 1450s, was a huge 900-tun ship that had cost Canynges £2,660. He is thought to have

purchased this particular ship in the Baltic. Another ship, the *Mary Canynges*, may have been named after his daughter. Headed by its founder, William Canynges, it employed 800 sailors and an additional 100 people in its shipyards.

6   In the 1450s and 1460s, a Canynges ship would regularly sail from Bristol to Iceland. Several merchants would consign cargo on board, and it would be traded almost entirely for salt cod and stockfish. Ships were getting smaller in the last half of the fifteenth century. By 1480 the 350-tun *Trinity* may have been the largest ship in regular use in Bristol.

7   A.E. Hudd, *Bristol Merchant Marks*, Clifton Antiquarian Society, Bristol, 1911. The many trademarks that have been catalogued in the last hundred years were mostly preserved in seals or recorded on documents used by the merchants.

8   Colon, trans. Keen, *The Life of Admiral Christopher Columbus*.

9   Ibid.

10   Ibid.

Four

1   Barrett, *History and Antiquities*, p. 170.

2   Anne Crawford, *Bristol and the Wine Trade*, Bristol branch of the Historical Association, 1984, p. 11.

3   T.F. Reddaway and Alwyn A. Ruddock, *Accounts of John Balsall, Purser of the Trinity of Bristol 1480–1*, Camden Miscellany XXIII, Royal Historical Society, 1969, p. 6.

4   Ibid., p. 12.

5   Newfoundland Heritage website (article by Wendy Churchill).

Five

1   Peter Fleming and Kieran Costello, *Discovering Cabot's Bristol*, Redcliffe Press, 1998, p. 14.

2   J.W. Sherbourne, *The Port of Bristol in the Middle Ages*, Bristol branch of the Historical Association, pp. 28–9.

Six

1 Peter Firstbrook, *The Voyage of the Matthew*, BBC Books, 1997, p. 113.
2 Sherbourne, *Port of Bristol in the Middle Ages*, p. 21.
3 Reddaway and Ruddock, *Accounts of John Balsall*, pp. 3–8.
4 Ibid.
5 Hudd, *Bristol Merchant Marks.*
6 For the accounts of Thomas Croft and John Wildegris, 29 September 1479–3 July 1480, see E.M. Carus-Wilson, *The Overseas Trade of Bristol in the Later Middle Ages*, Bristol Record Society, 1937. The Customs Records extant for this period record the dutiable imports and exports.
7 The *Trinity*, Lisbon to Bristol, arrived 4 March 1480

The Crew

Captain	Richard Parker
Purser	John Balsall
Ordinary seamen	18
Soldiers	8
Gunners	2
Cabin boys	3

Merchants	*Cargo*	*Totals*
	Wine	76 tuns
	Oil	182 tuns
	Salt	2 tuns
	Sugar	54 cwt
Robert Strange	Wine	
	Wax	60 cwt
John Pynke	Oil	
	Vinegar	
	Wine	
	Salt	

	Vinegar
	Misc.
Richard Amerike	Oil
	Sugar
William Bird	Oil
	Wax
John Esterfield	Oil
	Wine
William	Oil
Wodyngton	Sugar
	Wine

(Plus 92 others).

Carus-Wilson, *Customs Accounts*, pp. 260–4; Reddaway and Ruddock, *Accounts of John Balsall*, p. 15.

8 Reddaway and Ruddock, *Accounts of John Balsall*, p. 20. More circumstantial evidence came to light in the 1960s when some detailed shipping records prepared by the purser, John Balsall, of the *Trinity*, were accidentally discovered at the Mercer Company in Bridgnorth. Richard Amerike's name appears in bills of lading throughout these records in his earlier role as a merchant trader. These records, and the earlier Customs Records, produced a long list of merchants who specialized in the Spanish and Portuguese markets. When it was compared with the merchants who traded in the northern markets, very few names were repeated.

9 Donald Jones, *History of Clifton*, Phillimore, 1992, pp. 8–9. The date that John Broke and Amerike's daughter Joan acquired the manor (1470) is confusing, given the dates of their deaths recorded on their tomb in St Mary Redcliffe Church.

10 Peter MacDonald, *Cabot – The Naming of America*, Petmac Publications, 1997, pp. 43–4. Richard Amerike was most likely born either in Bristol or the Welsh border country that was voluntarily within English control. His Welsh father or perhaps his grandfather may have moved to Bristol or Monmouthshire

and registered the surname 'Ap Meric' with the authorities. If Richard Amerike had been born in West Wales, his father's name would have been Meric Ap (his father's given name). There would not have been a surname. Like the King, Amerike could also trace his ancestry back to the royal houses of Wales.

11 Richard Amerike was a direct descendant of Einion Yrth ap Cunedda, who was King of Gwynedd and Anglesey, in North Wales, in the fifth century. Einion was succeeded by Caswallon Llaw-Hir who ruled for many years until 517. This royal line continued through Maelgwyn Hir Gwynedd ap Caswallon, 517–49, Rhun Hir ap Maelgwyn Hir Gwynedd, 549–86, and Beli ap Rhun, 586–99. This lineage can be traced back even further to Beli Mawr, the King of Britain in about 100 BC whose son, Caswallon, was the general who opposed Julius Caesar's troops when the Roman army invaded Britain. In 1343, Elizabeth, also a descendant of Beli ap Rhun, married Sir John Poyntz, the wealthiest and most politically powerful person in the Bristol area at that time. Both Queen Elizabeth II and the late Diana, Princess of Wales, were descendants of the Poyntz family via their Tudor lineage and the Spencer family connections. Both Howel ap Meredydd and Elizabeth Poyntz share common ancestry with Richard Amerike.

12 In the late 1400s, Wales was a country that had been invaded and occupied by the English. The English authorities were administering the country and required everyone to register a surname, in English, to avoid the confusion that reigned. Many Welsh surnames date from that time, when the last name was anglicized and used thereafter by the family as its surname. Examples of this are Parry, which began as ap Harry, and Probert, which began as ap Robert. Welshmen who moved to England or lived in the border regions, or marches, faced this situation earlier. Amerike's father or grandfather may have moved to Bristol in the early 1400s, and the name was established when he registered his name with the authorities. It was subsequently anglicized. Thus, Ap Meric became Amerike.

13   Carus-Wilson, *Overseas Trade of Bristol* (quoted in MacDonald, *Naming of America*, p. 43).

14   Carus-Wilson, *Overseas Trade of Bristol*, pp. 245–80.

Seven

1   Calendar of State Papers Milan, London, 1912, English trans. A.B. Hinds; James Williamson, *The Cabot Voyages and Bristol Discovery under Henry VII*, Hakluyt Society, 1962, pp. 209–10.

2   Newfoundland Heritage website (article on sixteenth-century fisheries by Wendy Churchill).

3   Mark Kulansky, *Cod: a biography of the Fish that Changed the World*, Penguin, 1997, pp. 22–3.

4   The profits made by reselling dried salt cod in Spain and Portugal were much greater than those made by importing it to England. The mild climate and availability of fresh and salted fish from Ireland met most of the English market needs. However, the hot climate in some parts of Spain and Portugal and the doctrines of the Catholic Church meant that this market had virtually no fish supplies if dried cod was unavailable.

5   David Quinn, *England and the Discovery of America*, 1481–1620, Alfred, A. Knopt, 1974, pp. 48–55.

6   Williamson, *The Cabot Voyages*, p. 176 (quoted on the Newfoundland Heritage website).

7   For another exception, see Quinn, *England and the Discovery of America*. On one voyage of the *Christopher*, both William Spencer and John Pynke shipped fruit from Portugal to Bristol. (The *Christopher* would later achieve notoriety, in 1485, when it was captured by Inishbofin pirates off the coast of Galway, triggering an English–Irish diplomatic crisis.)

8   Carus-Wilson, *Overseas Trade of Bristol*. This marked the end of the Canynges Company's domination of Bristol business. William Canynges had died in 1474 at the age of seventy-five. He had no dependents, so his estate had been split up among his relatives. A year after his death, one of the Canynges fleet,

along with a relative, Thomas Canynges, fell into the hands of Breton pirates who demanded a ransom of £100. The family turned to Richard Amerike to borrow the ransom money. There is a record of Amerike later suing the Canynges heirs for non-payment of this debt. Amerike obtained the Canynges mansion on Redcliffe Street in settlement. The house was situated on the river near St Mary Redcliffe Church.

9 Quinn, *England and the Discovery of America*, p. 49. Amerike employed an Icelandic servant in his household as evidenced by a record of him paying a 2s 'foreign worker subsidy' in a census taken in 1485. There were forty-eight Icelandic servants in Bristol that year. But there is no record of Richard Amerike ever trading in the Icelandic market.

10 Basque fishermen may have established settlements in Newfoundland in the late 1400s, and Bristol merchant fishermen were there by 1481. A Danish sailor named Dietrich Pining also claimed to have discovered Newfoundland in 1472. In 1532, the French explorer Jacques Cartier planted a cross on the Gaspe peninsula in the St Lawrence River in Quebec and claimed it for France. He noted the presence of 1,000 Basque fishing vessels.

Eight

1 Treaty Roll 164 m. 10, Public Record Office, London.
2 Reddaway and Ruddock, *Accounts of John Balsall*, pp. 13–14; Patrick McGrath, *Westward Enterprise, English Activity in Ireland, the Atlantic and America*, ed. K.R. Andrews, Liverpool, 1978, p. 87.
3 List of Mayors in transactions for the year 1894–5, Clifton Antiquarian Society, Bristol Kalendars, pp. 124–31.
4 Wilson, *The Columbus Myth*, p. 61.
5 Quinn, *England and the Discovery of America*, pp. 50–5.
6 William Botoner (Worcestre), Williamson, *The Cabot Voyages*, pp. 187–8.

7 It is probable that this *Trinity* was not the 360-tun vessel that Worcestre wrote of in 1480 but was a smaller fishing ship that fit the terms of the trading licence, which limited the size of the ships to 60 tuns. Williamson, *The Cabot Voyages*, p. 189.

8 Reddaway and Ruddock, *Accounts of John Balsall*.

9 Wilson, *The Columbus Myth*, p. 62; Williamson, *The Cabot Voyages*, pp. 188–9.

10 Much has been made of the fact that Richard Amerike was not one of the jurors in Croft's trial or on the list of forty-four potential jurors. Before the trial started, he was selected to relate his knowledge of the case. He was later eliminated, suggesting he was an interested party. Straunge, Spencer, and de la Fount, the other three licence holders, were also eliminated from the beginning. Quinn, *England and the Discovery of America*, pp. 56–7.

11 When the trading licence expired in June 1483, the trade route to Brassyle was probably known by the Bristol merchants.

12 Merchant traders from Bristol had found the Island of Brassyle and the world's richest fishing grounds, situated 1,200 miles out in the Mare Oceanum. When Christopher Columbus heard about these voyages a few years later, it would be obvious to him that the Bristol fishing ships had, in fact, reached 'the northeast coast of Cathay'.

Nine

1 Archivo General de Simancas, in *Precursors*, trans. Biggar, 1911 (quoted in Williamson, *The Cabot Voyages*, pp. 228–9).

2 The Revd H.L. Thompson, *Poyntz Family History*, Cheltenham, 1879, p. 77.

3 Reddaway and Ruddock, *Accounts of John Balsall*.

4 Thompson, *Poyntz Family History*, p. 77.

5 December 1497, Calendar of State Papers Milan, London 1912, English trans. A.B. Hinds (quoted in Williamson, *The Cabot Voyages*, pp. 209–10).

6 William Adams, *Adam's Chronicle of Bristol 1623*, 1910.

7   Archivo General de Simancas, in *Precursors*, trans. Biggar (quoted in Williamson, *The Cabot Voyages*, pp. 228–9).

8   Amerike's annual salary was £6 13s 4d, a relatively small sum that was the equivalent of a skilled craftsman's wage. The position was an honorary appointment, and he was responsible for the collection of import taxes and Crown payments from revenues collected in Bristol. The Customs House, where he and his two bailiffs had their offices, was situated on the Broad Quay, where the larger ships tied up.

9   Robert, the eldest son of Robert Thorne, wrote to a Dr Leigh in 1514 regarding the visit his father and Hugh Elliot made to Newfoundland several years before the Cabot voyage (believed to be in 1494):

> '. . . this inclination and desire of this discovery I inherited from my Father, who with another merchant of Bristol, named Hugh Elliot, were the discoverers of the Newfoundlands, of which there is no doubt (as now plainly appeareth) if the mariners would have been ruled then, and followed the pilot's mind . . ., but the lands of the West Indies, from whence all the gold cometh, had been ours, for all is one coast as by the chart appeareth'.

The word 'discover' did not have the same meaning in 1500 as it does today. 'Visit' would be the equivalent term. Also, Newfoundland is used in a more general context. Thorne writes with some regret that they were in a position to sail further west and south along the American coast, but the crew didn't want to cooperate. Williamson, *The Cabot Voyages*, pp. 24–31.

10 Quinn's *England and the Discovery of America* discusses the written evidence for these Bristol to Brassyle voyages between 1480 and 1497. He examines the family ramblings of William Worcestre, the trial transcript of Thomas Croft, the letter of John Day, Pedros de Ayala's report to his government, and the letter from Robert Thorne.

11 Archivo General de Simancas, estado de Castilla, leg. 2. fol. 6; Vigneras, 1956 (quoted in Firstbrook, *The Voyage of the Matthew*, pp. 172–3).

Ten

1 *Journals of Christopher Columbus*, Hakluyt Society, 1893.
2 The ancient Romans named the Atlantic after the Atlas Mountains, which folded north-east-south-west along the western end of the Mediterranean Sea and marked the limits of the known world. The Atlantic lay 'beyond' the Atlas. In Greek mythology Atlas was a Titan god who fought an unsuccessful war against Zeus. Zeus punished Atlas by forcing him to stand and support the sky on his shoulders for ever. Atlas was portrayed standing on the north-west edge of the known world (Morocco) where the Atlas Mountains are today. (The theories of Eratosthenes 1,700 years earlier had been long forgotten.)
3 *Christopher Columbus, Age of Exploration, An Encyclopedia*, article by O.A.W. Dilke, p. 670.
4 Boorstin, *The Discoverers*, p. 247.

Eleven

1 Reddaway and Ruddock, *Accounts of John Balsall*, p. 27.
2 R. Katz, in *Christopher Columbus, Age of Exploration, An Encyclopedia*, p. 176.
3 Dyson and Christopher, *Columbus for Gold, God and Glory*, pp. 212–13.
4 R. Katz, in *Christopher Columbus, Age of Exploration, An Encyclopedia*, p. 182.
5 Helen Nader, in *Christopher Columbus, Age of Exploration, An Encyclopedia*, p. 188.
6 Dyson and Christopher, *Columbus for Gold, God and Glory*, pp. 65–79.
7 Reddaway and Ruddock, *Accounts of John Balsall*, p. 27.

Twelve

1 The story of Welshman Prince Madoc ab Owain Gwynedd's expedition and landing at present-day Mobile Bay in Alabama in 1170 has been discussed and debated for centuries, beginning with Hakluyt. Francis Bacon included it in a play in 1622. Donald McCormick, *Madoc and the Discovery of America* (1966), and Askew Roberts, *The History of the Gwydir Family* (Ruthin, 1827), as cited on website of Joseph Felcone, Booksellers, New Jersey www.felcone.com/amer

2 Richard Pflederer, 'Fernando Colon, Early European Adventurers and the Opening of Japan', in *Mercator'sWorld*, May/June 1996.

3 Samuel Eliot Morison, *The European Discovery of America: the Southern Voyages*, Oxford University Press, 1971, pp. 99–140.

Thirteen

1 Letters Patent, Public Records Office, Treaty Roll 178, Hakluyt's Voyages, vol. 3, pp. 5–6; trans. Biggar 1911 (quoted in Williamson, *The CabotVoyages*, pp. 204–5).

2 Archivo General de Simancas, estado de Castilla, leg. 2. fol. 6. Vigneras 1956. trans. Vigneras 1957; Williamson, *The CabotVoyages*, pp. 211–14.

3 Ibid. Day letter states that total complement was twenty.

4 Ibid.; also discussion by Morison, *European Discovery of America: NorthernVoyages*, pp. 206–10.

5 Williamson, *The Cabot Voyages*; Morison, *European Discovery of America: NorthernVoyages*, pp. 206–10.

6 Williamson, *The Cabot Voyages*; Morison, *European Discovery of America: NorthernVoyages*, pp. 206–10.

8 A.E. Hudd lecture, Bristol 1910.

Fourteen

1 Fernandes de Navarctte, *Coleccion de los viages y descubrimientos*, vol. 3, Madrid, 1829, p. 41 (quoted in Wilson, *The Columbus Myth*, p. 137; and Williamson, *The CabotVoyages*, p. 111).

2   Williamson, *The Cabot Voyages*, p. 88.

3   Ibid., pp. 110–13.

4   Fabian's chronicle as rendered by Hakluyt, *Divers Voyages*, 1582; Wilson, *The Columbus Myth*, p. 122; Williamson, *The Cabot Voyages*, p. 221.

5   The theory that one of Cabot's ships ran aground at Grates Cove, on the south-east coast of Newfoundland, originated partly because two Beothuk Indians were in possession of a broken sword and Venetian earring. Also, there was a rock into which Sancius Cabot, John's son, supposedly carved his name, IO Caboto and Sainmalia. In the early 1800s, it became a tourist attraction. It also drew thousands of birds, making it a less desirable destination. In the 1960s, the rock was stolen and disappeared in an American media van. It is now reputed to be in one of the Midwest states. Morison, *European Discovery of America: Northern Voyages*, pp. 203–4; and Newfoundland Heritage website.

6   Morison, *European Discovery of America: Northern Voyages*, pp. 188–90.

7   Archivo General de Simancas, Navarette; Williamson, *The Cabot Voyages*, pp. 228–9; Wilson, *The Columbus Myth*, p. 138.

8   Wilson, *The Columbus Myth*, p. 139–40.

9   Ibid., p. 137.

10 Boorstin, *The Discoverers*, p. 247.

11 Portolan World Chart, Juan de la Cosa, Cartographic Images website, slide 305.

12 In Vespucci's writings, this voyage of 1499–1500 was referred to as his second voyage. There is some dispute about whether he had travelled to both areas of present-day Brazil and South Carolina in 1497–8, as some accounts claim.

13 Williamson, *The Cabot Voyages*, pp. 118–28.

14 Looking at a map of the North Atlantic from the perspective of high latitude, it can be seen that a ship approaching North America from Great Britain would first encounter Newfoundland, and in circumnavigating the island, it would not be obvious that there was a large landmass to the west. The Grand Banks are south and east of

the island, and given the apparent wealth of the fishing grounds there, the Bristol fishermen initially had no need to go any further. It appears that they credited this island as being the Island of Seven Cities. They soon travelled further westwards, however, and apparently realized that the land to the west, which they called Brassyle, was a mainland of indeterminate size. The French also seemed to be aware of some of these developments. A map produced in Paris in 1490, two years before Columbus sailed to the Caribbean, shows a lone island in the Atlantic Ocean that bears a strong resemblance to the shape of Newfoundland.

Fifteen

1 *Mundus Novus*, Amerigo Vespucci (quoted in Wilson *The Columbus Myth*, p. 154).
2 Morison, *The European Discovery of America: Southern Voyages*, pp. 306–10.
3 Morison, *European Discovery of America: Southern Voyages*, ch. 12; and Boorstin, *The Discoverers*, ch. 33.

Sixteen

1 Customs Roll, Westminster Chapter Archives, Chapter Muniments; A.E. Hudd, *The Cabot Roll*, 1897.
2 Wilson, *The Columbus Myth*; Quinn, *England and the Discovery of America*.
3 Archivo General de Simancas, estado de Castilla, leg. 2. fol. 6, Vigneras, 1956. trans Vigneras 1957 (quoted in Firstbrook, *The Voyage of the Matthew*, pp. 172–3; Morison, *European Discovery of America: Northern Voyages*, pp. 167–88; and Williamson, *The Cabot Voyages*, pp. 211–14.
4 Williamson, *The Cabot Voyages*.
5 Ibid.
6 Ibid.

7   Ricart's Kalendar; Barrett, *History and Antiquities*.

Seventeen

1   The *Manorial History of Clifton*.
2   Peter Fleming and Kieran Costello, *Discovering Cabot's Bristol*, Redcliffe Press, 1998, p. 81.
3   *Medieval Monumental Brasses in St Mary Redcliffe*, pp. 11–13.

   The description of the missing brass is taken from Transactions at Bristol, the Manorial History of Clifton. John Broke was the son of Hugh Broke and the grandson of Sir Thomas Broke (1392–1439) of Holditch Court and Broke, Ilchester, by the heiress Cobham (Joan Baroness Cobham, Braybroke 1404–42) in Kent. Hugh Broke owned the Canynges mansion on Redcliffe Street, the same building Amerike gave to his daughter and son-in-law. The connections between the Amerike and Broke families appear to be numerous. The Lords Cobham were also descended from Sir Thomas Broke and included Edward Broke (1412–64), the 6th Lord Cobham and MP for Somerset, and another John Broke (1464–1511), the 7th Lord Cobham.

4   *Manorial History of Clifton*.
5   US flag website at usflag.org. Official Boy Scout Hand-book, United States flag code.
6   Sea traffic between Bristol and the American colonies, and later the United States, has been significant since 1600. Giles Penn, who came from Redcliffe, was a seafarer. His son, William, who was born in 1621, became an admiral. He was later knighted for his service to Charles II. William lent huge sums of money to King Charles, and on his death in 1670, his Quaker son, also named William, asked the king for repayment. Rather than ask for money, William asked for a grant of land in America to establish a Quaker colony. King Charles agreed as long as the land was called 'Penn' in honour of his trusted admiral, hence the birth of Pennsylvania. Admiral Penn is buried at the entrance of the south transept.

BIBLIOGRAPHY

Adams, William, *Adam's Chronicle of Bristol 1623*, Bristol, 1910.

Andrews, K.R., *Westward Enterprise, English Activities in Ireland, The Atlantic, and America 1480–1650*, Liverpool University Press, 1978.

Atlas of World History, HarperCollins, 1999.

Bantock, Anton, *The Cabot Story*, Redcliffe Press, 1997.

Barrett, William, *History and Antiquities of the City of Bristol*, Bristol, 1789.

Bartrum, P.C., *Welsh Geneologies AD 1400–1500*, National Library of Wales, 1983.

Bedini, Silvio A. (ed.), *Christopher Columbus and the Age of Exploration, an Encyclopedia*, DaCapo, 1998.

Biggar, H.P.,

Boorstin, Daniel J., *The Discoverers*, Vintage, 1985.

Brown, Lloyd, *The Maps and Chart Trade*, Dover Publications.

Carus Wilson, E.M. *The Overseas Trade of Bristol in the Later Middle Ages*, 1937.

Collinson, John, *History of Antiquities of the County of Somerset, 1741*.

Crawford, Anne, *Bristol and the Wine Trade*, Bristol Historical Association, 1984.

Dunning, Brian, 'The Man Who Gave America its Name', *Country Life*, 20 June 1963.

Dyson, John and Christopher, Peter, *Columbus for Gold, God, and Glory*, Simon and Schuster, 1991.

Firstbrook, Peter, *The Voyage of the Matthew: John Cabot and the Discovery of North America*, KQED, 1997.

Fleming, Peter and Costello, Kieran, *Discovering Cabot's Bristol*, Redcliffe Press, 1998.

Friar, Stephen and Ferguson, John, *Basic Heraldry*, Herbert, 1999.

Godman, Colin, *Lower Court Farm Archaeological Assessment*, 1990.

Bibliography

Hicks, Michael A., *Who's Who in Late Medieval England*, Shepheard-Walwyn, 1991.

Hudd, Alfred, 'Richard Ameryk and the name America' booklet published 1910.

——, *Bristol Merchant Marks*, Bristol.

Jones, Donald, *A History of Clifton*, Phillimore Press, 1992.

Keen, B., *The Life of Admiral Christopher Columbus by his son, Fernando Colon*, New Jersey, 1959.

Kulansky, Mark, *Cod: a biography of the Fish that Changed the World*, Penguin, 1997.

MacDonald, Peter, *Cabot and the Naming of America*, Petmac Publications, 1997.

Manorial History of Clifton.

Medieval Monumental Brasses in St Mary Redcliffe.

Morison, Samuel Eliot, *The European Discovery of America: The Northern Voyages*, Oxford University Press, 1971.

——, *The European Discovery of America: The Southern Voyages*, Oxford University Press, 1974.

Nebenzahl, Kenneth, *Atlas of Columbus and the Great Discoveries*, Rand McNally, 1990.

Prescott, F.H.M., *Once to Sinai*, Macmillan Co., 1958.

Quinn, David, *England and the Discovery of America* 1481–1620, Alfred A. Knopf, 1974.

Reddaway, T.F. and Ruddock, Alwyn A., *The Accounts of John Balsall, Purser of the Trinity of Bristol*, Royal Historical Society, 1969.

Sansom, John, *Bristol First*, Redcliffe Press, 1997.

Sherbourne, J.W., *The Port of Bristol in the Middle Ages*, Bristol Historical Association, 1965.

Siddons, Michael Powell, *The Development of Welsh Heraldry, Vol. II, A Welsh Armorial*, National Library of Wales, 1993.

Whitfield, Peter, *The Image of the World*, Pomegranate, 1994.

Williamson, David, *Kings and Queens of England*, Konecky and Konecky, 1998.

Williamson, James, *The Cabot Voyages and Bristol Discovery under Henry VII*, 1962.

Wilson, Ian, *The Columbus Myth*, Simon and Schuster, 1991.

WORLD WIDE WEBSITES

American Spice Trade Association: http://
http://www.astaspice.org/
www.astaspice.org/
Bristol, history of:
http://www.brisray.co.uk
http://www.brisray.co.uk
Contemporary maps:
http://www.henry-davis.com/MAPS
http://www.henry-davis.com/MAPS
Catholic Encyclopedia:
http://www.newadvent.org/cathen/
http://www.newadvent.org/cathen/
Cod trade:
http://www.bell.lib.umn.edu/Products/cod.html
http://www.bell.lib.umn.edu/Products/cod.html
Exploration and settlement of Newfoundland and Labrador:
http://www.heritage.nf.ca
http://www.hcritagc.nf.ca
The Matthew: http://www.matthew.co.uk/
Meyrick Coat of Arms and family history:
http://www.knighton.freeserve.co.uk/homepage/crest.htm
http://www.knighton.freeserve.co.uk/homepage/crest.htm
St Mary Redcliffe Church:
http://www.stmaryredcliffe.co.uk
http://www.stmarys.ebusiness.co.uk
Terra Incognita website:

http://www.ameryk.com
http://www.ameryk.com
US Flag: htp://www.usflag.org/
Waldseem‚ller maps:
http://www.bell.lib.umn.edu/
http://www.bell.lib.umn.edu/

INDEX

LIMEYS

ONE MAN'S WAR AGAINST PATRONAGE, IGNORANCE AND THE MOST DEADLY DISEASE OF HIS TIME

DAVID I. HARVIE

This is the dramatic story of the extraordinary heroic fight by one man to cure scurvy, man's first occupational disease which killed over two million men in three centuries. The cure led to the birth of the world's first soft drink, and an intriguing tale about why the English came to be called 'Limeys'.

DAVID I. HARVIE worked for the BBC until 1991. His *Lines Around the City*, an anthology on Glasgow, was published by Lindsay Publications in 1997. He lives in Dumbarton, Scotland.

12 B/W ILLUSTRATIONS
ISBN 0 7509 2772 0

HELIGOLAND

THE TRUE STORY OF GERMAN BIGHT:
THE ISLAND THAT BRITAIN BETRAYED

GEORGE DROWER

Britain swapped the small island of Heligoland in the North Sea, for Zanzibar in 1890, sparking a public controversy. After years of having a UK-style flag, postage stamps, taxation system and currency, the islanders were stripped of their culture, and were forced into learning German. The unscrupulous transfer of the island ultimately became a strategic blunder during the two world wars, when it was used by Germany as a base from which to attack Britain. Heligoland is now remembered daily in the Shipping Forecast as German Bight. This amazing story of intrigue, high adventure and national ambition highlights the evolving shape and identity of the British Isles.

GEORGE DROWER is an expert on overseas territories and author of the widely acclaimed *Britain's Dependent Territories* and *The Overseas Territories Handbook*.

16 B/W ILLUSTRATIONS
ISBN 0 7509 2600 7

LETTERS FROM THE MARY ROSE

David Loades & C.S. Knighton

The *Mary Rose* was Henry VIII's flagship, and served in the Royal Navy for thirty years before it sank during a battle with the French off Portsmouth in 1545. This book brings the story of one of the most famous ships in history vividly to life, aided by previously unpublished letters and documents including despatches written whilst the *Mary Rose* was on active service. Fully illustrated with pictures of artefacts recovered from the wreck.

Published in association with the Mary Rose Trust to mark the twentieth anniversary of the raising of the ship's hull in 1982.

DAVID LOADES is Honorary Research Professor at the University of Sheffield.

C.S. KNIGHTON is a naval historian.

12 COLOUR & 80 B/W ILLUSTRATIONS
ISBN 0 7509 2839 5

NEW WORLDS

THE GREAT VOYAGES OF DISCOVERY 1400–1600

RONALD H. FRITZE

New Worlds is a fascinating narrative history of the great voyages of discovery, and is the only book of its kind to span the crucial period 1400–1600 in one readable volume. The two centuries encompassed by this study are arguably the foundational years for modern Europe. The huge expansion in trade and the acquisition of vast empires which characterise the period set the pattern for at least the next 200 years. Drawing on new research into Columbus, Drake, da Gama and Cabot, among others, this is an up-to-date survey of an intrinsically exciting and interesting topic.

RONALD H. FRITZE is Chair and Professor of History at the University of Central Arkansas.

60 COLOUR & 50 B/W ILLUSTRATIONS
ISBN 0 7509 2346 6